A Return to Romance

Also by Michael Morgenstern

HOW TO MAKE LOVE TO A WOMAN

A Return to Romance

Finding It and Keeping It Alive

Michael Morgenstern

with Guy Kettelhack

HARPER & ROW, PUBLISHERS, New York
Cambridge, Philadelphia, San Francisco, London,
Mexico City, São Paulo, Singapore, Sydney

1817

A RETURN TO ROMANCE. Copyright © 1984 by Morgenstern Publishing Co. All rights reserved. Printed in the United States of America. No part of this book may be used or reproduced in any manner whatsoever without written permission except in the case of brief quotations embodied in critical articles and reviews. For information address Harper & Row, Publishers, Inc., 10 East 53rd Street, New York, N.Y. 10022. Published simultaneously in Canada by Fitzhenry & Whiteside Limited, Toronto.

FIRST EDITION

Designed by Lydia Link

Library of Congress Cataloging in Publication Data

Morgenstern, Michael.
   A return to romance.

   1. Courtship.   2. Love.   3. Dating (Social customs)   4. Love-letters.
5. Intimacy (Psychology)   I. Kettelhack, Guy.   II. Title.
HQ801.M77   1984   646.7'7   84-47591
ISBN 0-06-015350-4

84 85 86 87 88 10 9 8 7 6 5 4 3 2 1

To my parents, Carl and Marilyn Morgenstern,
whose thirty-four-year marriage speaks
for itself

Contents

Acknowledgments

W HILE THERE IS only one name on the cover of this book, my work would not have been possible without the help and encouragement of hundreds of people.

A book of this type is a distillation of the feelings and thoughts of men and women of different ages, backgrounds, and environments. Many of these ideas were born during discussions over coffee with friends, years before the notion ever crossed my mind that these ideas might be synthesized onto paper and read by others. Looking back now, I want to express my gratitude not only to those who gave their time and support, but to those who shared their valuable opinions as well. Each person, I believe, will recognize his or her particular contribution.

To name a few: Doris and Larry Ashkin, Jay Becker, Myron Beldock, Connie Clausen, Estelle and Paul Debbane, Florence and Abe Elenowitz, Neddie-Mae and Gene Elkus, Cara and Don Epstein, Perri Feuer, Errol

11

Frank, Ilene Freshcorn, Lynn Gansar, Roger Gates, Natalie and Jack Guttman, Brad Hamilton, Curt Hatfield, Liz Heimlich, Phil Heimlich, Justin Hirsch, Cheryl Hughes, David Korzenik, Barb Kramer, Craig Kridel, John Lazares, Marc Linowitz, Harry Lioce, Louise and Nick Lioce, Nicky Lioce, Roni Margolis, Bob Mazer, Nancy Morgan, Nachumi Olchik, Phyllis and Ralph Pagano, Steve Pechter, Wendy and Bobby Resnick, Carol and Steve Reubel, Brad Ruskin, Joe Scott, Semadar and David Shiff, Janice and Si Shulman, Sheila Sims, Whit and Ken Sims, Jane and Arthur Slaven, Marcy and Steven Slaven, Sue Hartman Slaven, Sy Slaven, Nancy Smith, Antonio Soddu, Susan and Claudio Stemberger, Andre Tavernese, Peg Tobolowsky, Sandy Trout, Tom Victor, Gail Canin Wilkins, Mitch Wilkins, Norma and Harry Wilkins, Fran and Steve Woolf.

Because I am not a member of the medical or psychiatric community, I am especially indebted to the many doctors who provided insights into a variety of areas drawing on their professional expertise as well as life experiences. Dr. Robert Wilkins, my long-time friend and a prominent medical doctor in New York City, was typically generous with his professional time and advice, in addition to sharing his particularly interesting insights into the nature of love and relationships. My mentor and friend Dr. Ed White, who is both a lawyer and a medical doctor, first pointed out to me the necessity of harmonizing one's life as a prerequisite to a good relationship. Finally, I was fortunate to meet Dr. Masao Miyamoto, a psychiatrist at the Cornell Medical Center in New York City, who is licensed to practice in both Japan and the United States; the sections of the book relating to international romance are in large part the result of talks with Masao.

Without the knowledge that I could, at any time, call upon a few very speical people, I would not have been able to finish this book. They are the few in my life who have taught me the lessons of love and friendship by example: Mom and Dad; sister Barbara; cousins Ilana and Hanania Bolchover; Terri Benjamin, Neddie-Mae Elkus, Arthur Slaven, Keiko Wakeshima, and Robert Wilkins.

At Harper & Row, I received the type of cooperation and support that makes the lonely task of writing less so. In particular, executive editor Lawrence Ashmead and director of publicity Dan Harvey were always there to encourage and assist me, as were associate editor Craig Nelson and editorial assistant Margaret Wimberger.

The winner of the award for patience and the ability to calm a sometimes too-spirited client goes to the Morton Janklow Literary Agency, with a special salute to Anne Sibbald. I also would like to thank Don Epstein and his staff at the Greater Talent Network lecture agency for their support and constant encouragement.

While my first book, *How to Make Love to a Woman*, was written from a man's point of view for men, *A Return to Romance* is written for both men and women. Two gifted associates, Karen Howell and Stacy Sims, provided the editorial creativity and commitment to this project that were necessary to balance many of the ideas presented. Karen and Stacy's research, dialogue, and editing were indispensable, as was the assistance of Guy Kettelhack.

A Return to Romance

1

Is Sex Enough?

"WHAT DO WE DO the ninety-eight percent of the
time we're not having sex?"

It's the most common question I've been asked, in
one form or another, in hundreds of letters and at the
dozens of appearances I've made across the country for
How to Make Love to a Woman.

In the last fifteen or twenty years we have all learned
about as much as anybody cares to know about sex.
We've learned theory from Masters and Johnson, posi-
tions from Alex Comfort's *The Joy of Sex*, and the phys-
iology of the "G spot" from Dr. Grafenburg. "Free sex,"
"Your place or mine?" and the "zipless f———" are
mere catchwords for the entire metamorphosis.

It's not that the "sexual revolution" didn't have
positive effects. It was successful in blasting myths which
once held us back: that men were automatically "experienced" and natural predators, and that women were passive damsels waiting for the phone to ring. Sex, before

the revolution, was some mysterious prize you were supposed to acquire only in marriage, when everything would be magically revealed to each of you. And sex certainly wasn't something you talked about in public.

Two decades have changed all this. We now have options we've never dreamed could be available to us; sexual and social horizons have widened to the vanishing point. Which is all to the good. Or is it?

Unfortunately, new myths have emerged which are as damaging as the old ones. First, anything that reminded us of the period prior to the late sixties and early seventies was automatically considered evil. This included any suggestion of "courtly love"—romance meant sexism.

Second, we entered an age of sexual Olympics. Performance became everything, and the pressure to perform (emotions be damned) was unprecedented. Suddenly technique and style in bed became the whole goal of any encounter, and the big O was all.

As I pointed out in *How to Make Love to a Woman*, sex by itself very quickly becomes boring. And all the sexual athleticism in the world will do very little to keep lovers together for more than a night or two. We all now know we need more.

But what?

That "what" is the subject of this book. The men and women I've talked to throughout the preparation of *How to Make Love to a Woman* and during the course of writing *A Return to Romance* are battle-scarred veterans of a sexual war nobody bargained for—a war not only between men and women, but within each of us. We no longer have clear models of masculinity or femininity to emulate, and the wide range of "relationship options" made available to us in the past fifteen or so years is as confusing as it was supposed to be liberating.

We ache for some clear solutions—ways we can find satisfaction in our love relationships—but we seem to have tried everything and nothing quite works. Our relationships have become graceless, self-conscious, and painful. A third of all marriages currently end in divorce. "Palimony" suits are slapped onto former lovers with greater and greater frequency. Scores of books and magazine articles try feverishly to teach us new sexual and social etiquettes, new techniques to "land and keep a lover." We've wrapped women in cellophane, tied aprons on men, handed out whips and chains, and sometimes even tried periods of enforced celibacy when it seemed there was no other way out. None of it has worked.

The collective and unmistakable message hundreds of men and women have expressed to me is this: we want to put grace, caring, and meaning back into our love lives. The answer isn't to return to the Dark Ages we so eagerly fled: luckily, we couldn't if we wanted to. The advances we've made in sexual equality are (fortunately) here to stay. But where have fun, affection, and security gone?

They've gone wherever romance went.

Romance is a term for which I'll shortly be providing a host of definitions, but it's sufficient to say here that romance is what we've lacked and what we want back. The problem is that most of us haven't a clue about how to do that—the very word "romance" conjures up a lost world of attitude and behavior, a world we may feel nostalgia for but have largely forgotten. Meeting students on college campuses, where I frequently lecture, has been a revelation: there is a whole new generation of men and women who have never known the art of conveying affection to a lover. They have nothing to remember.

There's a whole constellation of pleasures possible between a man and a woman—most of which occur long before getting to the bedroom. There's a delight in pursuing and in being pursued that we can learn to feel again. Millions of copies of "romance novels" in the bookstores and on women's bedside tables clearly indicate our starvation for that delight.

In the pages that follow, I hope to show you that you don't have to find romance vicariously in books or films or memories. You can bring it about in your own life— now. Most of all, I hope to convince men and women that they don't have to be afraid of one another. The cold war between the sexes is over. A new romantic world awaits you.

Join me in finding it.

2

Your Most Romantic Moment

THE ROMANTIC JOURNEY we'll be taking in this book is a varied one, with any number of surprising routes. But why take the journey in the first place? Because of the truth most of us have known—and suppressed—for a long time: we want to love and to be loved in imaginative, caring, romantic ways.

"Romantic." What does it mean?

Romance is a mixture of many elements combined in many different ways: it usually starts with good manners; it may take off into fantasy and often it's holding back so that whatever gesture you make to your lover has an unforgettable meaning.

But finally it's your own definition of romance which counts. The goal of this book is to lead you to this definition and to help you have the courage to develop the kind of romantic attitude which will allow you the best, most loving, and most exciting relationship you can have with another human being.

Hundreds of people I've talked to in the course of researching and promoting *How to Make Love to a Woman* have asked me to tell them how to get romance back into their lives. Here's the first step: start with your own experience.

What does romance mean—or what did it once mean—to you? I think the best way to find the answer is to take yourself back in time and ask: "What was my most romantic moment?"

There's no question I've enjoyed asking people more than this one, because everyone I've talked to loves to answer it. The hardest cynics soften, the shyest people open up. Something romantically special has happened to each of us. The look in the eyes of every man and woman I've asked to describe this moment has told me more than their words ever could: their "most romantic moment" was quite simply one of the best experiences they'd had—or could imagine having.

As you'll discover as you read on, Hollywood can in many ways help our love lives. But if you're like the men and women I've spoken to, your first time didn't resemble *Casablanca*. Bogart and Bergman may epitomize certain notions we have about romance, but most of the romantic experiences people have told me about didn't happen in exotic locales or unusual circumstances. The pure romance of the moment made people feel as if they were flying to the moon.

Marilyn, a beautiful, successful, and sophisticated woman in her early thirties, brought the truth of this home to me perhaps more vividly than anyone else.

Marilyn is a world traveler—her business takes her to Paris, London, Rome, and Tokyo almost as often as the rest of us go to the grocery store, and she's as comfortable on the Champs Élysées as she is on the streets of her Midwestern hometown. I looked forward to hearing about her "most romantic" moment, certain I'd be regaled by the plot of some exotic film script. As it happened, the only thing "far away" about Marilyn's tale was the look in her eyes.

"Tom," she said. "The boy who took me to my senior prom."

I was sure she'd misunderstood. "Your most, Marilyn—not your first."

"They were the same thing." She described Tom—and her feelings: "He was so nervous he nearly stuck me with the corsage. He stammered when he met my father at the door—he was so polite!" She drifted off a bit, smiling. "Everything he did—opening the car door, making sure I was comfortable, holding me so closely and gently when we danced, kissing me good-night—every single detail showed he cared. That's what was most romantic. I felt, for that night, like the most adored girl in the world."

Marilyn looked seventeen again, and I learned something about romance.

Romance in the memory and imagination is a powerful force. Your first and best romantic moments affect you far more deeply than you probably realize: they set up standards of romantic "success" to which you secretly (or unconsciously) compare all subsequent relationships. This doesn't mean that Marilyn won't be happy until she finds Tom again; but it does mean that the feeling she felt years ago with Tom is one she's cherished ever since, and one she's sought—consciously or not—in every relationship she's had since. Is this overlimiting? Unfair to all the subsequent men who aren't Tom? Marilyn doesn't think so—she feels lucky to know what real romance feels like, and she knows what she wants.

Romance involves imagination and fantasy to such a degree that your first romantic moment may not have happened with a "real" person at all. In quite a few cases, people told me they'd had two first romantic moments— the one dreamed about, and the one which actually took place. Marta, a woman from East Germany who now lives in New York, gave me her own poignant example of how this can happen. In her adjustments to a new culture and language, Marta has become one of the most practical and hard-headed women I've ever known, and so her dreamy, slightly wistful tone when she answered my questions about her first romantic moments surprised me. "Men don't realize how much time women spend fantasizing," she said. "Especially as a girl, I dreamed about the man I might one day meet and the life I would have with him. Even now, I find myself daydreaming in the most exact detail about meeting someone special, what he'll look like, what he'll say to me." Marta was amused by the look of incredulity in my eyes. She sensed how far this dreamy image seemed to me from the no-nonsense personality she usually projected. "I have never known a woman who didn't dream as I do about men and romance. And when a man embodies any part of those dreams, a woman is there for him."

Marta's "first time" happened largely in her imagination; she daydreamed about what she had little hope could happen in the harsh East German environment of her girlhood. But those dreams became her most precious possession, and when years later she finally met a man who treated her with some of the careful affection she longed for and had dreamed about, she was joyfully ready to respond—and return the affection she had hidden deep within her.

My definition of romance grew again. Like Marta, we all have very private romantic feelings and fantasies we carry around—at first not daring to think they could ever be brought to life. The reason so many people's first times were also their best times is because we're dazzled by the first experience of a dream coming to life. "Can this be happening?" we ask ourselves. "Can the romance we've always dreamed about actually be coming true?"

The point is that often we know much more about romance than we think we know. What Marta learned is that she could trust her fantasies to guide her to the "real" thing when the time was right. She allowed her feelings to become her guide.

Many of us don't trust ourselves to the same degree. I said at the beginning that I loved asking people what their first and most romantic moments were because everyone enjoyed answering—and that's true. But not everybody answered quickly. Quite a few people had convinced themselves they'd never known "true romance," that it was something which couldn't possibly happen to them. Life isn't some eternal movie set, I was told. Romance is fiction. "There's no such thing as a Prince Charming," said one woman.

I agreed that she probably was right, but when I got this woman to look a little deeper—when I coaxed her "first time" out of her—the man she described certainly sounded like a Prince Charming to me. This was the case with even the most outwardly cynical people I met: they eventually looked into their pasts and could find at least one glowing moment they cherished as their "most romantic." I've never seen so many surprised cynics! "Maybe I do know what romance is" became the collective response. "Maybe it is possible."

It's true that we're not helped to trust our own definitions and experiences of romance by the media which assault us daily. Look at the blurbs on any of the hundreds of romance novels you'll find in bookstores: "a steamy tale of fierce unbridled passion—lovers joined by a Fate no man or woman could resist," etcetera, etcetera. The mysterious dark men and impossibly lovely, willing women of these novels aren't anything that could happen to us, we think. And the bombardment of images of "perfect" men and women we get from advertising, television, and films doesn't persuade us that we could possibly experience "true" love or romance either. It's no wonder so many men and women haven't been able to answer the question "What is romance?" without saying it's something that happens to Richard Gere and Debra Winger. It's certainly not something that happens to the rest of us.

"Romance is best left to teenagers," said Sara, a forty-seven-year-old divorced mother of two. "They've got the time for it, for one thing. And they also have the illusion that it's possible." Sara's comment echoes so many other disillusioned men and women who spoke to me. It's a sad, if understandable, consensus. One typical response: "Look at the ads. Here's some gorgeous girl and guy in a perfect setting—no trappings, no context. How do they make their living? Don't they ever fight?

What happens when one of them gets old or fat or sick?" We look at these images with understandable frustration—and longing.

Again, it's no wonder that romance seems like some forever unattainable carrot before our noses.

However, what does Sara really mean when she says, "Romance is best left to teenagers"? How does she know that? What exactly is romance to a teenager? The only way we can answer that question is by looking into our own lives and allowing ourselves to relive the first glimmerings of love and excitement we felt as teenagers. You'll discover, if you reexperience this time vividly enough, that what happened to you then isn't nearly as distant as you thought it was.

One couple in particular illuminated this for me. Linda and David are a couple in their mid-twenties who admitted serious doubts about staying together. They were going through a rough time when I met them; I spoke to them separately. I think you'll be intrigued by what each revealed.

"My first romantic experience?" David thought the question pretty ironic, given the problems he was having in his current "romance." "Sometimes I feel like I've never had one at all. At least, it's hard to believe now." He took some time to think. "Okay," he finally said. "Yeah—there was a girl—and it was the first, maybe the best time. Funny"—he looked at me, his eyes brightening—"just remembering that time makes me feel better." It happened when he was a senior in high school, he told me, during spring break. He and some friends of his took off for Fort Lauderdale for a week. "I think every kid fantasizes about meeting the Perfect Person on that kind of vacation, and of course it usually doesn't happen. But it happened to me." On his first day there he met a girl from South Carolina, a beautiful red-haired, green-eyed girl who was a college freshman. "She seemed so much more experienced than anyone else I knew—it amazed me that she took any notice of me." They met on a beach, and to David's delight she agreed to meet him that night for a date. After a meal at a pizza joint, they walked for hours on the beach. "I can still smell and feel the air, hear the sound of the waves, feel the touch of her walking next to me," David said. "I had brought a bottle of wine—she was eighteen, after all, and I wanted to impress her with my sophistication." David laughed. "The problem was we couldn't drink it. I'd neglected to bring a corkscrew." "Mr. Suave" felt about two feet tall. "But she didn't seem disappointed at all," he continued. "I'll never forget the look in her eyes, glittering in the reflection of the moon, her laughing and—it was like she was asking me to hold her, telling me she thought I was somebody really special. The night was getting cooler; I put my arm around her, and we walked back to the boardwalk, and then back to her place. That wonderful look was still in her eyes, and she leaned over to kiss me good-night. That was it—just a kiss." David heaved a big sigh, then looked a little confused—then enlightened.

"You know what's weird?" he asked me. "All the while I was reliving that scene, another girl's face kept popping into my mind, replacing that South Carolina red-head. It was Linda's face."

I was trained as a lawyer, not a psychotherapist, but even I could see that David had made a helpful connection. What he may once have thought was a minor adolescent romantic moment now seemed to guide him, years later. He rekindled that "first time" feeling, and spontaneously it brought him to his current lover, Linda. Linda was all he could talk about the whole rest of the evening.

Amazingly, much the same thing happened when I spoke with Linda several days later. She was even more reluctant than David had been to discuss her "first time," but when I finally coaxed it out of her, she experienced the same transference.

For Linda it had been a winter scene, she a high school junior, her first romance a senior—walking in the snow, huddling into their coats and then into each other; Linda felt alive and warm and protected. She was even more explicit than David had been when she made her particular leap to the present: "The only other man I've felt that way with is David." She was thoughtful for a moment, then jumped up from her seat. "I've got to tell him that!" she said. She looked like nothing more than the sixteen-year-old girl she'd been her "first time."

I'm not suggesting we should conclude from this happy coincidence that all that troubled couples have to do is remember their "first times" to get together again. That it helped Linda and David to do so is as extraordinary as it is wonderful. But I learned a lesson from their dual confessions, and again I can add to our definition of romance.

Once you've felt the wonders of a "first time," you never lose that feeling. In fact, whether or not you're aware of it, the first and/or best romantic moment in your life becomes a sort of litmus test—a standard and a goal for you in all future relationships. It's not that we don't learn anything new after our "first times": we're always adding to our romantic lives, and in fact it's the goal of this book to show you how you can intensify your romantic life in ways you may never have dreamed you could.

But before we can define what romance is generally, we have to see what it means to each of us privately. All you have to do is look into your own experience, into your own heart, to find that definition. Trust what you find—let those feelings guide you.

Any advice or suggestions you'll find in the rest of this book are meant to do one thing, and one thing only: build on the feelings you already have, get you to trust them so you'll know whether anything new you "try on for size" fits you.

What was your first romantic moment?

Don't let anyone tell you that you don't know what romance is. You know better than anyone.

3

The Chase

Now THAT you've remembered the magic of your most romantic moment, how can you recapture that romance? You know perhaps better than you once thought you did the kind of relationship you're after. You may be trying to recapture the special feeling with your lover, or you may be "looking for love" from someone new. How do you meet that special person?

An introduction to anything—a book, a meal, a play, or a person—sets the tone for all that follows. First moments are important, even essential, to the success of what they lead to.

Knowing how to approach someone who attracts you isn't easy. You've all read the How to Pick Up books—or at least know they're out there—and you've all read or heard formulas "guaranteed" to work. If you're like me, you're wary of all these rules. I think for good reason.

First, we're not living in a time or culture which allows rigidity. Here's a brief history lesson from Reay

Tannahill, from her book *Sex in History*. It spells out something that you may already know—but in a surprising way:

> The people of medieval Europe had 12 generations during which to adjust to the idea that women were worthy of respect, the Victorians three generations to accept that they were worthy of the vote. The modern world has had to adapt to almost complete legal and sexual equality in less than a decade. Predictably, the results have been chaotic, and the psychological penalty is now having to be paid.

What is that psychological penalty? Part of it, writes Tannahill, is that "man lost his nerve . . . he began to go into retreat." Visualize this man and you'll come pretty close to Woody Allen, at least as he's portrayed in seventies movies.

The enormous social changes we've gone through in the past fifteen years or so aren't just grist for a sociologist's mill: we each have stories—sometimes horror stories—about our relatively new confusion with sexual and social roles. We don't quite know what a man or woman is supposed to do anymore. It can be a frightening world out there between men and women.

Men and women, as we've discovered, can and should find solace in memories of their first and best romantic times; but, considering the tug of war between men and women during the last fifteen years, it seems almost a miracle that we've had any romantic experiences at all! I can't tell you the number of times I've heard "I felt like such a fool when I called him" or "I seemed to have this uncanny ability to say exactly the wrong things when I met her"—amid hundreds of other tales of confusion, embarrassment, and woe. You've probably got a couple painful memories yourself.

It is harder to know what to do today than it was even twenty years ago. And any guide to "connecting" with the opposite sex, while it may contain pointers which might work in this or that circumstance, can't be considered a bible in times as unpredictable as ours. If you've read these guides, you know this all too painfully yourself.

It was hard, in fact, choosing the title for this chapter: "The Chase." It might sound like we're talking about hunting here—predators and prey. If there is a War Between the Sexes, shouldn't I hand out the weapons and ammunition?

I consider the initial moments between a man and a woman a "chase" in a far more gentle sense of the word. We chase after each other's hearts not because of some need to dominate each other or to win some contest, but because we see in the people who attract us a kindred spirit—something our hearts tell us to pursue. If you'd like a more old-fashioned word, call it courtship.

There are ways you can meet a lover without the two of you scaring the hell out of each other. But, as with finding your own definition of romance, you have to listen to yourself to find those ways.

I'm not saying you can't be bold. If it comes from the heart, imaginative boldness can be terrifically effective. What I'm talking about is attitude: a willingness to take the chance to be romantic and to see every opportunity as one that is potentially romantic.

Bob is a thirty-six-year-old stockbroker friend of mine who called me recently—I hadn't heard from him in some time, and expected he had something unusual to tell me about his work. He never seemed to have time for much of anything else.

"Hey, Mike?" He sounded bewildered. "You know what just got delivered to my door? A florist's box." This piece of information didn't strike me as all that unusual until I thought of my workaholic friend, and how he'd never given—or received—such a gift before. "You know what was in it?" He sounded like a little kid.

"Let me take a wild guess," I told him. "Flowers?"

"No!" he replied eagerly. "One flower. A single red rose." I asked him if there was a card too. "That's the most amazing part," he said. "It says, 'You are being courted.' Isn't that incredible? I mean, nobody's ever sent me flowers before." I'd never heard Bob use this tone. It was somehow joyful and heartbreaking at the same time. I asked him who signed it. He said nobody, but he thought he had an inkling who might have sent the box—and he hoped he was right. The secret suitor was a woman he'd wanted to meet for weeks but hadn't the nerve to talk to.

I secretly applauded any woman who could knock Bob's socks off romantically. Bob was so completely bound to his work, you needed a stick of dynamite to catch his attention. One rose had that effect. And not only did Bob's romancer catch his attention: she also snared his heart.

"You are being courted," the card said. Bob told me later the formality of the word "courted" touched him tremendously. In a single gesture this woman had been both surprising and formal—bold, spontaneous, and, in a lovely way, polite.

Her gesture also illuminates what we can use from what we may have thought was an archaic past. "Courtly love," as it came to be defined throughout the Middle Ages, had as its premise an adored and forever unattainable woman and an ardent, adoring lover who would all but lay down his life for his beloved. As you might suspect, this sense of courtly love had more reality in songs and literature than it ever had in real life, but the tradition created very strong images of women and men—images which influence us to this day. The ideal Victorian woman, many centuries after the ideal of courtly love first emerged, was still regarded as adored and unattainable and, above all, "pure." Relations—at least formal relations—between men and women in the nineteenth century were ritualized to a degree we would find stultifying today. You have only to glance at an etiquette book from the 1870s or 1880s to get a sense of the bewildering and rigid network of rules which regulated the behavior of men and women not so very long ago.

It's no wonder society chucked the whole thing out, right?

But let's go back to Bob and his ardent suitor—or suitoress. Despite the gender reversal, there wasn't all that much difference between the woman's wooing tactics and those of the quintessential Victorian gentleman. What thrilled Bob was the retrieval of the formal gesture. Bob, like many men who have received mixed and differing messages from women regarding the taboo of men and women treating one another differently, was doubly surprised when a woman went out of her way to treat him differently—and romantically. It woke him up.

Isn't that the goal of any first meeting or gesture? I'm not advocating that every woman who's interested in a man go out and send him a red rose and an anonymous card. The woman who did this for Bob did it because she sensed exactly what would work for him. Developing that sensitivity is what directs anyone to make the right first gesture.

As I've found out from dozens of people, there are any number of ways of sensitizing yourself to do exactly that. I've also heard a lot of painful stories about what doesn't work. It seems to me that every meeting that goes wrong—especially if the man and woman start out being attracted to one another—is an example of one or the other not taking the time to really see who else is there. We all send out cues. The trick is to pick them up.

Dr. David B. Givens, in his book *Love Signals*, talks about focusing on these cues: "Courting signs are multisensory and nonverbal the world over." Givens, an anthropologist, monitored the courting behavior of men and women in a variety of settings—offices, stores, singles bars, laundromats—over a period of years. He has done us the service of confirming—and codifying—what most people instinctively know and react to: we reveal ourselves every moment of our lives through "body language," even if consciously we think we're covering up.

For example, a man who feigns indifference to a woman who has just approached him will give his very real interest away by the tilt of his head, slightly shrugged shoulders, and stance. Dr. Givens tells us that this man is expressing one of the first stages of courting behavior—his body is interested even if his mind has decided to play it cool.

I'm not about to give you a codified list of body movements and stances which invariably mean yes, no, or maybe, because I believe you already instinctively know and react to body language. But the problem, again, is trusting that knowledge—allowing yourself to be directed by it. And decoding body language, while it's a tool to let you in on the real desires of someone you meet, isn't the only tool. In fact, if done too literally, reading body language can get you into trouble. I remember one friend who, having done his body-language homework in books and courses, decided that a certain woman he met at a party was crazy about him—her greatly dilated pupils and batting eyelashes made that all too clear, he thought. She excused herself for a moment—she had to go to the bathroom to remove her contact lenses!

The point is that there's no single set of cues you can rely on completely to clue into the moods and desires of someone you first meet—it's a question of sensing the whole person, of learning to allow him or her to come forth, and to see, on as many levels as possible, what's being expressed to you. This doesn't mean you should "lay back" completely—you can't simply become some passive sponge, absorbing "clues" until it seems right to make the first move. If you hang back too much you may find yourself talking to the air. Some courage is in order.

One of many tales of frustration pointed this out to me. In the months of research which went into this book, I received dozens of letters detailing "first times" and romantic successes and fumblings.

One man who wrote to me signed himself "Anonymous," which was all too poignantly appropriate, given the tale he had to tell. "You asked about people's first times and how they meet each other," he wrote. "My first times never seem to happen in the first place!" The example he described was typical, he said, of what happened to him with women. He lived in an apartment building a few doors down from a woman whose schedule closely matched his own: they left for work at the same time, returned at the same time, even seemed to do their laundry in the basement at the same time. He was crazy about her—it was a classic case of love at first sight. He even felt the attraction was returned—at least, he thought it might have been. That was the problem. She smiled and said hello when they rode the elevator up or down with one another—was she just being polite? Days passed; he knew to the minute when she'd be leaving her apartment for work—he'd listen for the click of her lock and "casually" emerge from his own apartment. He was so nervous about his "meetings" with her, however, that he became less and less able to imagine speaking to her, much less asking her out.

"Standing next to her was pure torture," he wrote. "Every time I opened my mouth to speak it seemed to be full of straw. I just couldn't get up the nerve."

Finally, it didn't matter anymore. "The woman moved out of town. How can I get over this shyness? This happens so often."

Shyness afflicts everybody to some degree, and never more than when we're with someone who attracts us—someone we'd like to impress. This anonymous man's shyness seems classic, but his fear can be expressed in very different, even opposite, ways.

The "masher" is in many cases just as shy as our anonymous friend. I don't think there's a woman I've talked to who hasn't had to suffer the attentions of a self-professed Casanova at a party or singles bar at least once. You know the guy: moving in with the grace of a rhino, bent on sweeping you off your feet with his savoir-faire and irresistibility. In fact, he's all too resistible. But scratch the surface of a Casanova and you may very well find the inscure soul of a Mr. Anonymous. What are Casanova and Anonymous afraid of, anyway? What are we all afraid of?

The most dreaded of all words: rejection.

I'm not about to give you magical tricks which will ensure you'll never hear the word "no" again in your life. There aren't any. Sometimes we come up empty-handed in "the chase," and it hurts. But minimizing your chances of rejection doesn't have to mean withdrawing like Anonymous or overwhelming your "prey" like Casanova. It gets back to the core of the best advice I can give: listen to yourself, and listen to whom you're with. It can take some soul-searching.

We're all masters of self-delusion. Sometimes we're attracted again and again to exactly the wrong situation or person; we often hit our own heads with a hammer. You don't have to be Freud to figure this out. One of my many correspondents, who's taught me more about romance and relationships than I could hope to find in a psychology textbook, bemoaned her tendency to meet Mr. Wrong:

> Meeting men isn't my problem. The problem is I always seem to meet the wrong kind. First there was a

man I'll call Jack, who was an artist—real sensitive—
who I met in a bar. That should have been my first clue.
He was a little drunk when we met, but that just made
him seem more charming and vulnerable to me. I'm not
sure who was the moth and who was the flame but we
seemed to burn each other up fast. He was wedded to
drinking and I was wedded to some vision of him as a
"vulnerable man." I guess I was the moth. I got burnt
and left alone while he went on drinking.

This woman went on to recount other experiences, if
not with alcoholics then with similarly crippled men, all
of whom she was attracted to because she thought she
could "mother" them, change them. Not one of them did
change, however, and she finally accepted that the only
person she had a hope of changing was herself.

I've tried to figure out why I've been so attracted to
weak men. I'm still not sure but part of it seems to be
that I want someone to take care of me. I guess I've
never felt I was worth that kind of caring, and so I've
just reversed things. But at least a warning bell rings.
now when I meet someone like Jack. I've discovered
that the kind of man I've always been attracted to just
isn't right for me. That's a start, anyway.

It's more than a start, I think. It's about the most important insight she could come up with: she discovered
ways in which she sabotaged herself, and she's made the
healthy decision she doesn't want to do that anymore.

My advice may sound awfully general: first you have
to figure out who you are; then you have to understand
why you're attracted to a certain breed of man or woman.

This I know for sure: the problems between men and women start when these general principles are neglected.

What are some specific ways of allowing a first meeting to work?

First of all: respect whom you're with, starting off with physical respect. I'm not about to tell you that grabbing someone you're attracted to and have just met isn't a particularly wise course of action—you know that already. What I'm talking about is a little more subtle, and I go back to Dr. Givens's *Love Signals* for a terse explanation of it.

The cliché phrase "You're invading my space" points to a real, annoying truth. Most of us have an invisible shield which maps out our personal "territory." Dr. Givens cites studies that put the perimeters of that shield at eighteen inches—a kind of bubble of space we don't want violated without giving permission. Is there anything more annoying than somebody who puts his face three inches in front of yours and jabbers away at you? This may seem like a superficial problem. It's not. Because you're doing more than violating physical space when you "take over" in this way. You're emotionally dominating your "quarry," with the clear message that what you have to say is a lot more important than what whoever you're talking to has to say. Moving in like this also isn't erotic, and if that's a concern you have in a first meeting with somebody who attracts you—keep your distance. Let your eyes caress before you let your hands or face wander in.

Second, don't be afraid to be polite. Try a little formality. I've discovered a deeply hidden secret—one that I'll have to divulge very carefully so that you won't think

I'm trying to drag us all back to the Dark Ages. The re-sounding message I've got from the women I've talked to—even the most outspoken feminists—is that they don't, after all, mind if a man helps them into a coat, opens a door for them, brings them flowers. In fact, the real secret is that women love this kind of attention! And men, with their fragile egos and little-boy souls, don't mind a little attention either, even if it means nothing other than a woman allowing a man to play the Old-Fashioned Suitor.

Although the previous couple of decades helped men and women gain equal ground in many areas, many of the discarded values are those which made the chase just plain fun. We threw the baby out with the bath water. Gestures of social etiquette are not political statements; rather, they are expressions of common courtesy and in many ways serve a very valuable social function: legitimizing touching. And it is the touch—the handshake that lasts a bit too long, for instance—that instantly lets a woman and a man know if the chemistry is there.

As we saw before with my stockbroker friend Bob, those formal attentions don't have to come from the ex-pected or conventional masculine source—but it's okay if they do. The secret basically is this: women and men do want to be treated a bit differently. A man may have the best of feminist intentions and treat a woman like "one of the guys," but he'll probably find that a gentler, even chivalric, approach will appeal to a woman as a first ges-ture a great deal more. And it isn't politically incorrect for a woman to allow a man to treat her with deference.

You can't create romance by treating a first meeting as a board meeting; rather, your first gesture, the way you approach somebody who attracts you the first time, needs a bit of magic as well as sensitivity. And sometimes that magic comes ready-made in the most formal—even most conventional—behavior. It's not that you have to tip your top hat or curtsey like an ante-bellum Southern belle, but it's not a sin if you do. In fact, by practicing a few 1980s equivalents, you'll stand the best chance of winning the heart you want to win.

Now that we know how to listen, how to sense the whole person, how to act on what we sense with a little restraint and a lot of affection, and can feel the promise of "something more": now that, in short, we've succeeded in this first crucial meeting—what next?

Romance is like a plant: it requires careful nurturing to bring it to bloom. And, as with certain especially fragile plants, bringing romance to fruition is an art. You've planted the seed, now it's time to coax the first growth. How?

Read on.

4

The Lost Art of Dating

"NAH, I don't have anything to do—you can come over if you want."

Sound like one ten-year-old to another on a boring Sunday afternoon? Actually, that invitation was one grown man's version of dating, complained twenty-seven-year-old Kathy, a woman fast becoming disenchanted with her boyfriend of six months, Greg. Greg was astonished when Kathy told him several days later, "Things aren't working out."

"Don't people do anything together anymore?" Kathy pleaded with me. "Greg couldn't get over the fact that I didn't want to 'hang out' at his place watching television. He said he felt so comfortable with me just doing nothing. I guess he meant that as a compliment, and I suppose in some way it was one. But I felt about as special as a well-worn rug."

We may have learned the fun—even the success—of

"the chase," but too often after the first rosy mist lifts, and we've caught the "right" person, the relationship grinds to a halt. Suddenly there's nothing to do. We put our "prizes" on a proverbial shelf and let them become tarnished. One day our precious prize disintegrates before our eyes, rusted with neglect.

Romance is an art that must be consciously and continually practiced and polished—and dating, the old-fashioned, somewhat formal, but delightful custom we all seemed to embrace enthusiastically as teenagers, is one of romance's most effective mediums. But we're not seventeen anymore. Adults don't "date" now, do they? Sure, you may catch a movie or a meal or take a walk, but you wouldn't call that a real "date," would you? Not if you know the person. Things are more casual now.

Even if you've just met someone, isn't it outdated to ask for a "date"? Annette Funicello and Frankie Avalon "dated"; but these are the 1980s. We're all too sophisticated for that stuff now. We may "get together" if we want, but it's nothing to make a big deal out of.

Lesson number one: start making a big deal out of it.

A date is an assignation, a rendezvous, an event, an occasion. It's one of the most exciting, pleasurable, downright wonderful activities you can share with another person. Whether it's a first date or a seventieth (yes, you can "date" each other even when you're married—I know a lot of people who do, and that's what they call it too), a date succeeds when you and your lover use it. "Use" it?

Kathy sensed that she and Greg weren't using their time together in a satisfying way for both of them. They may have spent time together, but it wasn't time which brought them closer; to Kathy it was "dead" time. It wasn't enough that they were "fond" of one another—you can be fond of an easy chair in that sense. We all change moment by moment, and a relationship is healthy—and exciting—when it embraces those changes. Romance can ensure that you constantly see your lover in a fresh light, and dating is one of the most effective romantic techniques for doing just that.

Unfortunately, it's an art most of us have lost.

Some men recognize that a date—and exactly that, one date—is "appropriate behavior." But once is rarely enough.

Sandra, a thirty-two-year-old hairdresser who lives in Atlanta, wrote me about a terrific first date, one she hadn't a clue would happen—she didn't expect to meet Jeff the way she did. In fact, the entire scenario was a little awkward, Sandra recalled with a hint of embarrassment. Sandra's friend Jenny, who is always on the lookout for "available men," was dining at an elegant hotel one night when she noticed the restaurant's maître d', Jeff. The next day Jenny reported to Sandra that Jeff was more handsome than Robert Redford, Tom Selleck, and Paul Newman combined, and that Sandra just had to see him. Sandra didn't consider herself a man-chaser (and she knew Jenny's penchant for hyperbole); however, she convinced herself she would try the restaurant with her friend because she "wanted to see what the food was like."

Instead she saw what Jeff was like. Jenny hadn't exaggerated: Jeff was gorgeous. When Sandra said she innocently caught his eye, Jeff returned the look warmly.

Jenny caught their exchange and sighed. "Well, I guess you're the lucky one," she said, conceding defeat. "But you'd better tell me everything about him when you get together!"

Sandra was embarrassed. "We haven't even met yet!"

Soon enough Jeff made their meeting happen by ordering after-dinner drinks for the women, compliments of the house. "Perhaps he'd like to join us," Jenny told the waiter encouragingly. Waiting for just such an invitation, Jeff did join them, and, as Jenny conveniently left the table for the women's room, he wasted no time in asking Sandra out.

Their first date was a brilliant example of romantic engineering. It was mid-summer, and Jeff knew a secluded spot in the country with a makeshift stone barbecue—perfect for a private picnic. He'd brought along everything—food, wine, even a spray of flowers, which he put into a container of water and carefully placed in the center of their picnic blanket. He was fascinating— alive—and as witty as he was handsome. Sandra's breath was taken away. It was a perfect date.

Unfortunately, it turned out to be the only real date Sandra and Jeff had. Not that Jeff didn't call—he did, usually late at night and at the last minute, asking Sandra to come over for a beer and "sit around." Sometimes, as a real "treat," Jeff invited Sandra to the hotel restaurant. But more often than not during those "dates" Jeff ignored Sandra while he joked with his cronies at the bar. Sandra was an attractive woman, and apparently once Jeff felt he had captured her, all he wanted to do was show her off, like some merit badge. All the charm he exuded on their first date disappeared into thin air. Sandra finally did too.

Sandra quickly realized that Jeff viewed their first, wonderful date as a duty—a job he had to do to get the girl. Admittedly, that technique worked in the short run. Even when Jeff got into his rut of "non-dates," Sandra didn't give up immediately. She kept thinking, if only she initiated something really spectacular—like hang-gliding together—Jeff would start paying attention to her again. But every time she called with such a plan, he said he was "too tired" to do more than drink beer with Sandra and camp out in front of the television set.

Kathy and Greg—Sandra and Jeff. I could tell you a dozen similar tales. The lesson is this: courtship that stops after the initial stages of a relationship spells almost certain disaster; couples miss out on the fun, the closeness, they would share simply by deciding to do something together. "As Time Goes By" is the quintessential romantic song from the quintessential romantic movie, but its lyrics—"and man must have his mate"—don't tell you that "have" means love.

I've suggested—and I will continue to suggest—that romance can be especially successful when a man plays the traditional suitor. It's not a sin for a man to adopt some of the tried-and-true courtship traditions with women. I'm not suggesting this out of the blue—so many women have told me they're delighted by these attentions. I don't believe it's a male prerogative to "capture" a woman and then take her for granted. In fact, it's one sure way to lose her.

The question of prerogative surfaces time and again

in the modern-day dilemma of who's supposed to ask whom out. As you read this book, a new type of "women's revolution" is taking place. Women are developing their own, unique style of active courtship, completely different from the no-frills, come-get-me assault of the 1970s, and equally different from the passive, damsel-in-distress prototype of old. The process of developing a space-age courtship ideal is a slow one. But I believe that in the not too distant future, there will be a return to *vive la différence*. Getting there may take some time, but it's where we're going. Enough with theory; what should we do now?

It's true that today many women feel comfortable asking a man out. In a previous chapter, we saw how effective a woman who initiates courtship can be (it was Bob who got the rose, not the other way around). Still, with hundreds of years of tradition and conditioning, a lot of women just don't feel comfortable making the first move. "I know it's supposed to be okay for me to call a man," one woman told me. "So why do I feel so uneasy every time I do it?"

Many—if not most—of the women I've interviewed still would rather have a man make the first move. I'm not saying it's right or wrong or that this is the way things will always be. But most women simply expect men to make the first move, despite the women's liberation movement. Men, though, don't seem to have recovered from the last fifteen years of receiving mixed messages from women. "Why are men so shy?" was a frequent complaint from women. "It's like they think we'll jump down their throats if they open their mouths."

Remember our social historian Reay Tannahill? "Men have gone into retreat."

Men get sweaty palms dialing the numbers of women and so do women. I've discovered that much of the problem with dating is that men think first dates have to be conventionally "romantic." A date has to be on a Friday or Saturday night, it has to include an expensive stop at a restaurant; the man feels he must perform as a dazzling conversationalist and a promising lover. With these kind of expectations, it's no wonder "men have gone into retreat." Or women, for that matter.

I implied at the beginning of this chapter that the whole concept of "dating," at least as it was understood in the heyday of Dick Clark and American Bandstand, is as extinct in most of our minds today as dinosaurs. And indeed, we affect that sophistication. But there's a deeper truth. One of the reasons we're so quick to declare dating dead is because a date still implies formality—and we're afraid of formality.

It's true that recent social changes have resulted in "role confusion"—men are afraid women won't stand for traditional "macho" behavior, even something as relatively benign as Acting the Suitor on a dinner date. Women also keep wondering what it is they're supposed to be and do. One of the secrets I've uncovered is that men and women don't know what a date is supposed to look, feel, and sound like anymore.

Here comes the good news. Dating is a lot easier than you think. And it's a lot more fun than you may have imagined.

A date doesn't have to be a hot-and-heavy Saturday-night confrontation. It can happen on a Tuesday morning. Why not ask the person you want to ask out to breakfast? One couple I know in New York had their first date at the Waldorf—he asked her out to an early breakfast, leaving enough time for them to languish over coffee together before starting work. That's sexy. (They weren't wealthy either—breakfast at a fancy restaurant is a lot cheaper than dinner.) Their next date was at the equally fancy Plaza Hotel—the following Tuesday at 7 A.M. They got to know one another in very romantic environments, but without the pressure that often attends a "will she or won't she" late-night weekend date. Of course, they did eventually graduate to weekend evening rendezvous when they were ready. By that time romance had blossomed to where they had no doubts about spending time anywhere with one another. But it began in the morning, before work, over eggs and coffee.

Make your first date a real activity. Again, it can happen in the middle of the day—an amusement park, a tennis game, even a game of pool or darts! What many people I've spoken to fear the most about a Big Date is having to sit over a table and talk "meaningfully." I'm all in favor of meaningful talk, but I also know what the tension of a first meeting with an attractive somebody can feel like—you can try so hard to impress that you'll find yourself choking on your tongue. A shared activity—and a sport is a good one—helps to defuse the tension. You can sometimes express more through what you're doing together than you could trying to spill it all out in words. The best date means joy in being together: do whatever it is you both like, and let the look in your eyes (and maybe the swing of your tennis racket!) speak louder than your first words could.

Activities which bring you together are obviously best for a date. One couple I know met in New Haven, Connecticut—at a library. He saw her first, and was immediately attracted. He noticed what she was reading—Emily Dickinson—about whom (although he liked poetry) he knew almost nothing. He quickly found and leafed through a collection of Dickinson's poetry, liked it, but had questions about it. He sat down at the same study table as the woman, and passed her a note. "I'm having trouble with her punctuation," the note said. "Why all those dashes?" She read the note, looked up at him, blushed slightly, and then smiled with real pleasure. She picked up her books, motioned for him to "come on," and they went to a nearby coffee house to discuss Dickinson. And of course in the guise of discussing Dickinson, they discussed themselves.

This last example points out something to do with spontaneity. I've said that many men and women fear Dating with a capital D because it can seem so planned, such a calculated event—and fear and expectations can shoot up to the bursting point. It's true that it's difficult to make a date without actually setting one, but you can take cues from any moment and turn an unplanned meeting into a "date." That's what the man in the library did to meet his Emily Dickinson woman; the sensitivity we've talked about before—an essential component of romance—emerged at exactly the right moment here. The idea came to this man spontaneously, but carrying out his introduction took some careful—if quick—planning. This is the essence of any successful date—seizing whatever moment you've planned and turning it into a caring gesture.

Except for the first, unfortunate couples with whom I began this chapter, we've concentrated mainly on the first dates—the truly planned moments a man and a woman spend with each other. But dating shouldn't stop—and it doesn't have to.

I've met a number of married couples who've turned dating into a romantic routine, which, with all the importance I've given to spontaneity and breaking ruts, might sound like a bald contradiction. But it isn't.

One working couple in their late thirties, who live in Cincinnati and have been married for twelve years, have a regular date—every Wednesday night at their favorite Italian restaurant. This is their special time alone, a time they can count on, and a time they reserve completely for themselves. They rarely even vary what they order—the waiter knows them so well by now that a mere nod is sufficient to tell him that they'll be having "the usual." They are left alone—the staff smiles warmly at them when they are seated. I'm astonished when I see them there. The obvious love they feel for one another makes them seem like newlyweds.

A routine can be very romantic too.

In fact, my neighbors have followed one simple one, which I'd taken for granted because I was so used to it— until I realized, writing this book, how romantic it really is. What do they do? Every evening around dinner time, I can look out my kitchen window and see them taking a walk. No big deal. But, on the other hand, they've been married over thirty years.

There are so many ways to bring dating into even a long-term relationship. One of the simplest is to call any meeting you plan to have with your lover a "date." If you plan to meet for lunch don't say something like "Hey, meet you for a bite at Joe's." Ask your lover if he or she would like to join you for lunch—for a date.

It's amazing how good that can make a hamburger taste.

5

The Equally Lost Art of Writing a Love Letter

JOHN NAISBETT, the author of the best seller *Megatrends*, devotes an entire chapter to a subject one might not expect in a book about business and technology: "High Tech/High Touch." Naisbett's theory is that "the more high technology there is around us, the more there's a need for human touch."

Naisbett's chapter may seem unrelated to a discussion of one of the loveliest ways a man and a woman can communicate—through the written word. But bear with me. In his book Naisbett identified a need for human intimacy, even in the context of technology. Such an emotion is closely akin to our own need for romance.

The advent of fast, high-tech communication threatens to drive the art of writing a love letter into oblivion. The telegraph, the telephone, and the telex (in the order of their invention, if not importance, here—the telephone is the real villain in this story) have made writing all but obsolete. Through a quick series of monosyllabic grunts, a message that once took careful and thoughtful composition now can be unceremoniously blurted out over a wire in a split second.

Of course, there are many differences between writing a letter and speaking on the telephone. But the main, romantic, difference is this: you can hold a letter, savor it, cherish it for all time. Try accomplishing that with a telephone call!

Not everyone subscribes to my theory that "letters are better." The grande dame of etiquette, Amy Vanderbilt, thinks love letters are dangerous admissions of emotion. Letters, Ms. Vanderbilt said in her book *Etiquette*, are "bombshells. . . . Nothing should go into a letter that couldn't be read in court."

The lady may have a point, and the lawyer in me understands. But there will always be dangers inherent in revealing emotions and affection in any form of communication, written or otherwise. It seems to me—and to the many people I've talked to who've held onto letters for years and years—the downside is heavily outweighed by the pleasures. What worries Ms. Vanderbilt is that letters are commitments.

That's what delights me.

Let's get back to grunts on the telephone versus a carefully worded sentence. I'm not going to give you a course in Creative Writing 101, so the first thing to make clear is that you don't have to be an Elizabeth Barrett Browning to "count the ways" you love someone on paper. I'm not going to attempt to teach anyone how to be "literary." But I do believe that a simple, sincere line or two committed to paper can say infinitely more than an hour and a half of "How are you?" and "I'm fine" on the telephone.

I speak from experience. I once knew a lovely high-fashion model whose assignments took her to every exotic spot on earth, far away from me. The memory of my phone bill after two weeks of calling her every other day when she was in Tokyo on a job still is crystal-clear. But what she later told me she cherished most of all was a short note I penned to her one night when I was particularly lonely. I don't think it said much more than "I miss you so much; all my love . . . ."

I met her eagerly at the airport when she finally returned. She came off the plane beaming. "What a lovely letter!" were the first words she said to me.

Not a word about the dozen phone calls.

A letter can be a real gift, a tangible "gesture," one experiences long after the words have been written. "A personal letter," wrote Ronald Varney in an article in *Esquire* magazine about the art of writing a letter, "can bring out the self in a way that is not always possible in person." What can a letter do that a "live" voice can't?

First of all, when you write, you can't rely—as you can with your voice—on a pause, or a rise in volume, or a lowering of pitch to convey your full meaning. Writing a letter means re-creating the nuances of your voice on a page. You've got to allow your reader to "hear" you through the written word. Perhaps that's what makes a letter so special. Enthusiasm we'd unthinkingly express vocally, sorrow or loss which would be obvious from tone of voice, sensuality which we'd have no trouble expressing over the phone or in person, all take a bit more effort when we communicate by pen. And such expressions often have a lot more impact in writing.

Another reason I'm not as worried as Amy Vanderbilt about the potential volatility of a letter is that writing takes more thought and a more conscious choice of words than those you might unwittingly let loose in conversation.

Admittedly, some people are better at—or at least more at ease with—writing a letter than others. One poor soul, a man named Bill, told me about his girl friend, who wrote him frequently from college—frequently and beautifully. She went on for pages about her moods, her life, and her feelings for him. Her letters were so vivid he felt he was actually physically with her when he read them. The problem was he was intimidated about responding. He wasn't any literary whiz—how could he possibly match her performance?

She kept asking: "Why don't I ever hear from you?" He was at college too, and their schools were hundreds of miles apart—he couldn't afford frequent phone calls. On the rare occasions he did call, he tried to reassure her: "Don't worry, I'll get a letter out tomorrow." But he never did. Every time he sat down to try, everything he wrote looked and sounded dumb. He even had lousy handwriting. Sometimes he'd say, "What the hell," and actually get a paragraph or two out, stuff it into an envelope, even address and stamp the envelope. But he could never bring himself to drop it into the mailbox. He was sure she'd laugh at his feeble efforts.

If it hadn't been for Bill's roommate, his girl friend might never have received more than a monthly call from Bill. Quite innocently, his roommate picked up one of the stamped but never-meant-to-be-sent letters from Bill's desk. He was going to the post office anyway; he thought he'd do his roommate a favor and drop the letter off for him.

Later that day he told Bill the favor he'd done him. Bill nearly collapsed. "How could you?!" he shouted at his bewildered friend.

"Well, it was stamped, wasn't it?"

Bill was exasperated. "Just because a letter is stamped doesn't mean it's going to get mailed, damn it!"

"Oh," replied the baffled roommate.

Bill was sure that this was the end of his relationship with his girl friend. He was mortified, especially when several days later he found a message taped to his door that she'd called. "Here it comes," he thought.

But he drummed up his courage and called her. Maybe he could apologize for being such a fool.

As you no doubt have predicted, Bill's girl friend was ecstatic. "I never knew you felt that way about me!" she said. "It was the most beautiful letter I've ever received."

How well Bill's letter was written from a literary perspective wasn't, of course, the point. It was the fact that he'd written at all, and that his words came from his heart, which won this particular woman's heart. As carefully composed as a love letter may be, it's even more carefully read.

Actually, "carefully read" doesn't begin to say it. Cheryl, a girl friend of mine from years ago and a good friend now, recently surprised me with the contents of a shoe box she'd held onto since our college days. Guess whose letters were in that shoe box!

Of course I was flattered she'd saved them, but I was

also surprised. I asked her why she had hung onto them after so many years:

"Because they were part of my life," she said simply. "Rereading them brings back so much, not only the things you wrote about, but where I was when I read them. I remember reading so hard between the lines it was as if you'd said fifty times as much as you actually did!"

Reading between the lines is exactly what we do with love letters. How I remember poring over letters from girl friends long ago, trying to tease out the exact meaning of the simplest sentences! "I can't wait to see you in June," wrote one girl. "Let's see, now," I thought, "can she really not wait? What does she mean 'see'? Doesn't she want to do anything else? No, she wouldn't put that in the letter. But does she really feel the way about me I feel about her? Is she happy meeting me in June? Why didn't she say the end of May—I mean, she could get here a week earlier, couldn't she?" And so on.

No piece of writing receives the kind of scrutiny a love letter does.

Love letters don't have to be limited to starry-eyed college students, either. There are times when writing a letter to a lover you've lived with can say more than hours of talk. Again, a letter takes time and requires thought. A woman named Shirley wrote me from Oregon about her "letter-writing relationship" with her husband, Harry.

Shirley is a busy housewife; Harry runs a clothing store in Portland. Before she begins her day, and after Harry has left for work, Shirley will often sit down with a cup of coffee and take out paper and pen. It's time she takes for reflection, but it's also time she allows herself to say the things to Harry she's wanted to say but feels more comfortable about revealing on a page.

"I think better that way," she wrote me. A typical letter might begin: "I was thinking about what you said last night, Harry . . ." and then she'd offer opinions and observations about any number of things—how her husband's business was going, the pros and cons of buying a new house, ideas for a vacation, why they may have disagreed about this or that topic. "Nothing very profound," wrote Shirley, "and sometimes I wouldn't need to show Harry the actual letter. It sometimes was enough that I'd thought something through for myself." But Harry liked receiving her letters. They were always loving expressions of her thoughts, real attempts to share her feelings with him. And reading them allowed him unaccustomed time to reflect, to plan, to muse.

"I don't usually let it get around that I write letters to my own husband," Shirley continued. "I guess it does sound kind of nutty. But they really work. We're closer for it."

What shouldn't you write in a love letter?

You'll remember the story about that terribly shy man who couldn't bring himself to speak to the attractive woman in the elevator. I was reminded of that man when I received the following letter from one correspondent, a woman named Caroline, who lives in New Jersey:

> . . . I had a pen pal once, and he taught me all the things never to do in a letter. I was given his name from one of those computerized dating services where they match you up with someone they think is compatible

with you. Well, Tom seemed compatible on the face of it. I liked the beach, and classical music, didn't smoke, am in my mid-twenties, and Tom was apparently all of those things too. But unfortunately he wrote the most boring letters!

Caroline was quick to point out that she wasn't being a literary critic; it was just that poor Tom never managed, although he wrote pages and pages about his activities, to say one truly revealing thing about himself.

His letters were like résumés. "First I did this and then I did that and then I did that and next week I'm going to do this . . ." It's like he'd turned his whole life into a laundry list, and what he had to say was about as interesting.

Caroline was particularly unhappy that he never responded to any of things she wrote to him about—she tried to draw him out with her letters, but he seemed incapable of taking the hint.

She ended her letter to me:

I almost laughed when I got his last letter. He said, "Now that we know each other so well, don't you think it's time to meet?" I replied as politely as I could that I was afraid I didn't feel the right chemistry. What I felt was this: even if he couldn't put together a grammatical sentence but still said something which meant something a little personal, a little teasing, a little human, I'd gladly have met him. But I couldn't envision a real person writing all those lists.

That's the key.

A letter which speaks directly, warmly, and, above all, honestly is the letter that gets read and reread and cherished. And it doesn't have to be long.

One of the delightful things a man and a woman can do via the mail is to keep a private, even "coded" conversation going, an exchange based on some secret only they share. A letter is never more intimate or effective than when it carries that kind of secret message.

One couple I interviewed had this down to a real art.

Anna is an advertising copywriter and Dan is a restaurant owner in nearby Santa Barbara. They see each other as often as they can, but sometimes work keeps them apart for weeks at a time. Quite spontaneously Anna started up an imaginary suspense tale about a nurse who meets a lawyer in Paris; they have an affair, and then get embroiled because they find a rare manuscript by Shakespeare in a Left Bank flea market, and various unsavory types are after their hides in pursuit of it. This brief description of the tale doesn't begin to do it justice, but what Anna and Dan have done with it is fascinating. Anna started a game, after they'd spontaneously come up with their outrageous plot one evening on the phone, by sending Dan a cryptic card with a picture of the Eiffel Tower on the front. "You be the lawyer, I'll be the nurse" was all Anna wrote on the card, signing it, "Love, A."

Dan quickly followed suit. "Meet you at the usual place on the Boulevard Champs Élysées" was all his card said, though he signed it, "Panting, D."

Soon their post cards—each carrying a picture of something crucial to wherever they were taking the plot—flew back and forth every day. Anna and Dan were particularly delighted to do all this on post cards any mailman could read—they secretly hoped they were baffling the whole Los Angeles postal staff!

The written word is a powerful tool, and whether it appears in a Christmas card, a scribbled note, or a six-page letter, it can be one of the most effective romantic tools any lover could possibly use.

Remember that the best letters aren't always the best written. The best letters contain at least one telling detail—one memorable message which means something surprising and special to the person who writes it and the person who receives it.

What should that message ultimately mean?

The three most important words a man and a woman could possibly say to one another. I'll give you a clue. The second word is "love."

6

Kissing

EVERYONE LEARNED how to kiss in high school, didn't they? What more is there to say?

A lot!

Maybe kissing hasn't been as good since, but it was sure terrific back then. And almost every woman I've spoken to—and every man who has been open enough to admit it—longs for the "rush," the excitement and romance of their first kiss.

You cannot have a first time more than once. But, you *can* re-create the electricity.

Your first kiss. You remember. What was it about the first time?

For me it was a warm June night. I was fifteen, so was Susan. I'd never met anyone like Susan. I'd spent months of freshman year in high school just looking at her, trying to drum up the courage to talk to this blond, wonderful girl. She seemed to float, not walk. When she was called on in class, her quiet voice could have been music. When I finally asked her (mumbling) if I could borrow her algebra notebook for an evening because my notes didn't make any sense and she was so smart, and Lord knows what else, she said, "Sure!" And she smiled at me. Her notes didn't make much sense to me either that night. I could only think of the girl who'd written them.

When the impossible happened—on the last day of school I asked her if, uh, she liked music, because there was an outdoor band concert the next Saturday, and, uh . . . and she said yes— I felt I'd conquered the world! She wore a pale blue dress that lightly clung to her, her long blond hair was pulled back in a pony tail, and she smelled of violets. She was the most beautiful girl I could imagine, and here she was sitting next to me.

The band played for her; the night was warm for her; it seemed to be June for her. I walked her home slowly after the concert. I didn't want this moment to go away. We walked through the village park, accidentally brushing against each other in the dark. That brief touch made me bold. I reached for her hand, and held it. She didn't say a word, but she kept her hand in mine. My body was trembling so much it was a wonder I didn't trip over her. Her house was just on the other side of the park, facing it—already it had come into view. I couldn't let her go yet. We came to the edge of the park, the soft June breeze rustling the leaves of a sycamore which sheltered us. A little light from a street lamp filtered through, highlighting her hair, her eyes, as I turned to her. She looked at me, and smiled. She allowed my face to come close, and we kissed.

Susan and I spent the rest of the summer with one another. The first shyness gave way to a gradual getting to know each other. We kissed all the time. A good-night kiss always lasted at least an hour, usually both of us standing on the front porch, leaning against the house, and in each other's arms. Romantic? Yes. No words can really describe what we felt and learned in those months. I'll remember Susan for the rest of my life.

We did learn how to kiss back in high school. But somehow we've forgotten.

Most of the men and women with whom I've spoken bemoan the "death" of kissing; the intimacy and excitement they felt the first time seem to have become ancient history. What was once the most wonderful communication they could imagine between a man and a woman now has become as mundane as a limp handshake. Or worse, a kind of sexual come-on, with no other purpose than to get to the "good stuff." Men and women have lost kissing, and they want it back.

Laura, a sophisticated woman of thirty-five and an advertising executive, once married and now divorced but with no want of suitors, voices a typical complaint: "Men have forgotten how to kiss. Apart from a dutiful little peck or, just as bad, a man lunging at you with a 'French' mouth, I can't remember a man who really knows what kissing is about. Now it seems if a man bothers to kiss you at all, it's something to get out of the way. But what he's getting out of the way is the most beautiful part!" Laura's voice quieted. "I won't say I got divorced from my husband because he wouldn't kiss me. But not kissing was an emblem of something more deeply wrong. A kiss is an approach, something a man can do for a woman to show he cares, and to set the stage slowly for the love-making to come. So few men seem to understand that."

Bob, a lawyer friend of mine, tells quite a different story: "I really looked forward to my first evening with Karen. She was gorgeous, and she seemed so self-assured, which is always a turn-on for me. We had a nice dinner out, I took her home. She invited me in for coffee. We'd barely gotten past the front door when she spun around and looked me in the eyes, as though she were accusing me of something. 'Well?' she said. 'Go ahead! Don't be shy.' Up until then, kissing her was very much on my mind."

Tom, a stockbroker on Wall Street, related an equally disappointing experience, one which was the opposite of Bob's "accuser." "I went out with a woman who was so intent on being feminine, which I guess she seemed to think meant utterly passive, that kissing her was like kissing a bowl of warm Jell-o. There was no resistance, no hint of passion. Just a complete 'Take me.'"

What's gone wrong?

What's gone wrong is that the sexual revolution in many ways focused us on performance and sexual intercourse only. Most men and women want more. They want the message of affection and caring that any type of touching should convey—but especially the kiss. A lover who is dissatisfied with his or her lover's kissing most certainly will be dissatisfied with whatever happens after the kiss. What Laura objects to about a man who pecks at her or lunges at her like a Buick with its hood open is that he is telling her, "Let's get the preliminaries over with."

Laura doesn't want a kiss to be a "preliminary." She wants something more: that is, that the kiss carry the same message that she expects from all her lover's actions—that he cares for her. Bob was stopped cold by Karen's "Go ahead" challenge because of what he took to be her real message: "You might as well kiss me. Isn't that what you're here for?" Bob told me he'd been ready for anything at the beginning of his date with Karen—anything but her icy challenge.

Bob's story points out something else. Karen's challenge was also bad timing. Kissing is not only communication, but communication which happens at the right moment. Romance is the art of holding back. Nothing benefits more from holding back than a kiss.

Theresa, a legal secretary in her mid-twenties, told me about her lover, Howard. "He's not exactly Robert Redford. In fact, he probably comes across downright plain to most people. But I've been hooked on him ever since our first kiss." Theresa was already glowing with whatever memory this stirred up. "It was as if he knew just the right moment to—I don't know—approach me. We'd gone out a few times, met for lunch during the week since we worked in the same neighborhood, and what I didn't realize then but now can see is that he was leading me. We did nothing but shake hands the first couple times, but I can still feel the gentle pressure of his fingers. It's silly, I know, but it's almost like *that* was our first kiss."

I asked Theresa to explain what she meant by Howard "leading" her. She searched for the right words. "It's as if every single thing he did, opening a door for me, asking me how my day was going, even just smiling at me, all showed me he really cared about me. The way he just barely touched me as we walked down the street, reaching for my hand just as we parted, and always—maybe this is the most important part—looking into my eyes as if he really wanted to . . ."

"What?" I egged her on.

Theresa laughed. "Kiss me, I guess And when he did, it felt like the most completely right moment in my life."

What Theresa didn't tell me is how Howard kissed her. It was enough for her to say that he did. There was no need to say more.

A kiss is a gesture which speaks. It isn't some strategic maneuver but rather a message that conveys, "I care about you more than I can say." Many times the message will be spontaneous. Other times you earn the moment by carefully building up to it. Whether planned or quixotic, a kiss must be allowed to happen, never forced.

We've forgotten that kissing is an event, a celebration of attraction. The technique, or what you do to convey the very special message that you care, doesn't matter nearly as much as most people think. Every case of "bad" technique I've heard from the people I've talked to boils down to a far different problem. Bad technique is merely a man or woman or both interpreting a kiss as a means to one end—having sex. But kissing is an end in itself. It needs nothing more.

Anyone who views the simple touching of another person as something remarkable and wonderful in and of itself will quickly learn to kiss well. I'm convinced we don't need more guides which tell us how to tilt our heads so that we don't bump noses. I didn't need to take Kissing Technique 101 for my first kiss, and I'm sure you didn't either. We learned in different, more subtle, ways, with our hearts the guide.

But before we throw technique out the window, it may help to redefine it less clinically—and more romantically. Mark and Nancy are two good friends of mine who have been married for seven years. Nancy speaks for both of them: "Mark and I went through what I guess are the usual ups and downs of a relationship which lasts longer than two years. I won't say the honeymoon was completely over after those first twenty-four months, but I wasn't thinking up too many 'creative' ways to please him anymore, and he wasn't either. What both of us had let up on, for sure, was kissing. It just didn't seem necessary. I mean, we were married, not courting. But I really missed it even if I didn't feel I could tell Mark. It seemed he'd lost interest completely.

"One night—we'd been married about three years— we were giving a buffet dinner party for more guests than we usually have, twenty or twenty-five. It was mid-January, the coldest part of the winter, and just stuffing everybody's coats into the closet was a lot of work! I remember lumbering down the hall with a raccoon coat and three down parkas. As I stuffed them into the closet I turned around to see Mark utterly covered with his own load of fur and down (half our guests had arrived at once), blocking my way. This bearlike creature let out a long, low growl, which I took to mean he wanted help with the load. I started to pull at a parka. He wouldn't give it up.

We got into a tug of war. We were like two kids suddenly rolling around on the floor in this sea of coats! Out from under a peacoat came Mark's goofy face. He kissed me, totally without warning, stopping my laughter with a long, deep kiss. God, it was wonderful!"

Nancy went on to tell me of a number of other odd-ball kissing "events" Mark staged afterwards. Not too many, Nancy was quick to assure me. The fun was how unexpected it was. She still doesn't know what got into his head to bring kissing back to their marriage. She's only glad he did. "And now, more often than before," Nancy confided in me, "we even kiss like they do in the movies! And that's wonderful too."

You won't find Mark's approach to kissing in any of the Love Guides I know. Mark somehow learned that as much as a kiss must happen at the right moment, it must always carry that tiny element of surprise: "This is new!" The best kiss is always, *in some way*, a first kiss.

The secret of the best kissing is simple. Allow what you *feel* to direct what you *do*. There are no magical techniques which will always work. Allow whatever you do to be a response to the moment, a moment you're sharing with another person. You don't kiss alone. It's an intimate moment you share.

Communication, timing, imagination, sensitivity, and sharing. Kissing should include all of these things, and yet there's more. What is that last magical essence, the thing that makes kissing wonderful, when it is? I don't know that anyone can describe it. But it has to do with a kiss being a kiss even when it isn't. If there's one thing I've learned from all the tales I've heard, it's that the brush of a hand, the "embrace" of someone looking deeply into your eyes, can mean every bit as much as the meeting of each other's lips. Sometimes it can even mean more!

7

The Fine Art of Resistance

"**B**UT YOU had such persistence, you wore down my resistance," croons Linda Ronstadt in her remake of the torch song "I've Got a Crush on You." Ms. Ronstadt, alas, pines over a delicious predicament that is all too rare these days.

So far we've seen that romance includes that art of resistance—holding back just enough, waiting until exactly the right moment—so that a question, a reply, a kiss, love-making can be as exquisitely satisfying as possible. Unfortunately, nowadays we rarely recognize the art of resistance. As the old song goes, you need a "persister" before you can have a "resister." When the most romantic question we grapple with is "Your place or mine?" the setting is not too conducive for seduction.

Resistance is at the heart of romance because it requires us to take our time. Sometimes we need time to decide if we want to get involved. Sometimes resistance creates the "exquisite time" needed to fan the flames of a fledgling romance. There's also a third kind of resistance that needs to be recognized: the "no" that really means no. You can learn to sense when resistance will heighten romance in your life, and when restraint will help you make a graceful exit out of a relationship.

We'll learn about many uses of resistance in the following chapters. But the concept is so essential to romance that it's necessary to attempt to define it broadly before we go applying it. What about the first kind of resistance: allowing yourself time to decide whether you want someone to become your prospective "significant other"? A delightful caricature of a woman who effectively employs romantic restraint is played by Claudette Colbert in the movie *Bluebeard's Eighth Wife*.

The plot centers on Gary Cooper, a millionaire whose hobby is collecting wives. He typically marries a woman who momentarily catches his fancy, makes love to her, gets bored, divorces her and goes on to the next. He hasn't, however, reckoned with the character played by Claudette Colbert, his potential eighth victim. Ms. Colbert sweetly obliges Mr. Cooper by marrying him—and then spends much of the rest of the movie avoiding the consummation in hilarious but seductive ways until Gary Cooper's eyes are opened to the fact that she intends to be his eighth—and last—wife. Cooper, unaccustomed to rebuff, is driven wild by the lady's "No, not yet" taunts. By the movie's end, he's chased her until she has caught him.

We may laugh at the 1930s world that made this kind of pursuit and frustration possible. But we can use the principle employed by Claudette Colbert today.

Let's start with "blunt questions."

The 1980s species of sexual predator often poses an indelicate question: "Wanna go to bed?" This question allows two and a half answers: yes, no, and maybe. If the question is asked by someone you find unattractive as well as blunt, you'll have no problem answering no. But what if, maybe, you are attracted—but think it's too soon to jump into bed? In that "maybe, but not now" response lies a whole world of romantic options.

Here's the story of a woman who handled this beautifully; she gives us the key to what romantic resistance is all about. Dorothy is an exceedingly attractive woman I met when she approached me after a lecture I gave at a large Southwestern university. I'd been talking that night about "Love in the Eighties" and how we couldn't be blamed for not knowing the best ways of holding back in a relationship because we hadn't been taught to value restraint. Dorothy particularly was intrigued by this problem, and she told me how, in one circumstance, she instinctively seemed to know how to handle herself.

"There's an incredible pressure to 'make it' here," she said. "From the first day of freshman year on, there's a tremendous pressure to spend the night in some boy's room. It's like a rite of passage. But I noticed something about the girls who won that prize. Sure, at first they walked a little more confidently than the rest of us—as if they were terribly sophisticated, grown-up women—and they got the usual round of questions from their close but still 'inexperienced' friends—what was it like? etcetera. Having sex seemed like getting a merit badge." Dorothy creased her brow. "But you could tell afterwards that something wasn't right about it. There was a look in every 'experienced' girl's eyes I saw of 'Is that all there is?' It was a little sad to see."

Dorothy decided to err on the side of restraint and she held back.

"Some guys I knew right off I'd never consider going to bed with. There are a lot of grabby frat men on this campus." But finally Dorothy met a man two years older than she was, and the chemistry clicked. When the inevitable question came, she sensed he felt embarrassed and shy. She said she suddenly got her first insight into the game both were playing. "I realized that he was under the same pressure I was to have sex—maybe much more. Suddenly it all seemed so silly to me, trying so hard to find a man to have sex with so that you could be 'in.'"

"No," she told him gently, "I don't think we're ready for it." The man didn't try the usual lines calculated to persuade—how meaningful their encounter would be, how intimately they could get to know one another. He just looked at her with gratitude and, Dorothy was intrigued to notice, a touch of relief. "It wasn't that he wasn't attracted to me," she continued, "but I felt he was a little relieved that he didn't have to prove himself to me. He did something which made me feel closer to him than sex could have at that moment—he talked to me."

It was difficult for Dorothy's man to admit that he was tired of the sexual-conquest routine, but he told Dorothy about his feelings because of the way she said no. Dorothy quoted him: "I've wanted to get to know you more than any other girl I've seen on campus. In a funny way, I think I was hoping you'd say no. Because I wanted whatever happened between us to be really special—I wish I'd had the guts not to ask you the big question, but I'm glad you've given us both some time."

Dorothy's no had a variety of meanings. She was able, by looking into this guy's eyes, by touching his hand as she answered, to say yes to a future with him and no to rushing into something which might endanger that future. She remembered walking back to her dorm late at night, after spending hours with this very special man. She walked into her room; her roommate looked up, eyes bright, and asked, "Well? Did you?"

"I did a lot of things tonight," Dorothy replied, smiling.

We've already learned that a first date on a Tuesday morning may be a more successful way of getting things started than a first date on a late Saturday night. Dorothy discovered that the payoff for relaxing and enjoying the person who attracts you—rather than jumping into bed— can far exceed one's expectations.

In fact, holding back romantically can be a lot of fun, and keeping your lover temporarily at bay can be amazingly erotic. This is the second type of resistance I mentioned at the outset—making the waiting sexy. A word which has received a good deal of unwarranted bad press best describes this process: flirting.

Flirting should be the "maybe" promise of "might deliver." This doesn't mean that every time you catch the eye of an attractive somebody on a bus, smile, and say hello that you have to jump into bed with that somebody because that's what you're promising—we've already seen with Dorothy that that doesn't have to be the case. It's honest flirting that I'm talking about: a seductive introduction whose main purpose is to say, "Hey, you're a very interesting person; I'd like to get to know you." What makes flirting fun is the degree to which you imply that message of interest—make it clear that your eyes are lighting up for a reason, but keep that slightest interest a secret.

Eyes that link "across a crowded room" say many things you want flirting to say: "You are incredibly attractive, I've never felt this way before, I'm a little frightened. Should I come over to you? Would you please come over to me?" The "who asks who" dilemma intensifies in a flirting situation, and the best flirting balances self-confidence with shy beckoning in a subtle mixture of yes and no. To flirt means to tease, but with the seductive promise of "not yet." That "not yet" becomes "soon." And that "soon," finally, at just the right moment, becomes "yes."

What a lovely journey it can be to that yes!

Resistance, again, is the key, and I remember the first time I learned its power. I once had a girl friend whom I took to the most romantic restaurant I knew—an old-fashioned "Continental" place with ballroom dancing, of all things. I wasn't exactly up on the fox trot, but I hoped that the candlelight and the ambience of the place would compensate for my two left feet. I was incredibly attracted to this woman, whom I had met only recently. She had long, thick, dark hair and she seemed mysterious in a kind of Mediterranean way.

After several glasses of wine, which eased our self-consciousness, my hand "naturally" found hers at one moment. What I remember about that first touch is how she withdrew her hand at exactly the right moment. That touch—and its withdrawal—was one of the most erotic experiences I can imagine having at a dining-room table! Later, when we danced, she continued her gentle resistance. My impulse was to draw her near, but every time my arm tightened she seemed to float away. The image I have of her dancing was one of a flowing spirit, sometimes here, sometimes there, always just out of reach. The touch of my hand on her waist became wonderfully erotic because I felt that at any moment she might withdraw from it. Her eyes were laughing and just the slightest bit distant—beckoning but mysterious.

By the end of the evening she had me terribly intrigued. And yet all we'd done was dance.

Romantic resistance is a fine art because it means walking a fine line. The crude flirt all too often is just coy or, worse, dishonest. We all have stories of "teases" and "mashers" who both have unfairly given flirting a bad name.

As we'll see even more clearly in the next chapter, trying too hard to be "open" or "up front" can spell romantic tragedy. Flirting means holding back, stirring the imagination, saying maybe before saying yes.

The art of resistance is well worth learning. Whether it's resisting the temptation to declare undying love mere seconds after you've met someone, or creating distance between yourself and a lover in order to magnify the intensity of the inevitable but delayed consummation of passion, the creative and careful maybe will lead to a glorious and much welcomed yes.

The power of that delayed yes has never been captured better than by James Joyce at the end of *Ulysses*. Listen to Molly Bloom:

And then I asked him with my eyes to ask again yes and then he asked me would I yes to say yes my mountain flower and first I put my arms around him yes and drew him down to me so he could feel my breasts all perfume yes and his heart was going like mad and yes I said yes I will, Yes.

8

To Tell the Truth

Probably the most difficult problem in nurturing romance has to do with honesty. Is it always the best policy? Can you tell too much?

The call to "let it all hang out" is one vestige of the sixties and the seventies which continues to infect people like a plague. With the best of intentions, people bare their souls in minute detail and find themselves talking to the air. Why? Don't people want to know everything? Isn't it healthy to put it all on the line? If you feel something, why not say it?

The current belief that candor is automatically a virtue has a history familiar to most of us. First there was Freud, and analysis. Certainly the Victorian heritage we'd been saddled with—keeping a stiff upper lip, holding it all in, keeping one's head at all costs—needed a stick or two of dynamite, and Freud provided the explosion. But gradually talking to an analyst wasn't enough; opening the doors to your inner psyche and letting the demons out, but keeping them within the book-lined room with the leather couch and bearded psychiatrist, apparently wasn't letting them out enough. The encounter groups, consciousness-raising, Happenings, Gestalt, EST, and sex therapy we've experienced in the past fifteen or twenty years have let our inner demons run amok in the most public of places. It can now be dangerous to ask what was once a polite question: "How are you?"

Too often we're told too much.

What people have forgotten in the series of "let it all hang out" explosions we've gone through is that honesty doesn't have to mean blurting out the truth in whatever way it comes to you. Honesty involves choice. You don't choose to express your feelings to a brick wall; you choose to express them to another living, breathing human being, with all the sensitivity and feeling you have inside yourself. And you can choose, in telling the truth, to be kind.

Andy and Margaret are two lovers in their late twenties who'd been with one another for over a year when I met them, and the story Andy told me about their first anniversary of a few months before is as revealing as any I've heard about the use, and misuse, of "utter honesty." The upcoming dinner, Andy said, couldn't have been a happier evening to look forward to. They felt more in love with each other than at the beginning, and Andy even felt the time might be right to talk about marriage. It promised to be a special night.

"We were still living in separate apartments then," Andy said, "and Margaret made dinner at her place. I was nervous: it almost seemed like this evening was the first time I'd seen her. She was beautiful, and she'd obviously gone to great pains to make everything perfect. She seemed nervous, too, but in a different way than I felt. It was as if she were on the verge of bursting out with something terrible. She finally did.

"'Andy,' she said to me, 'there's a lot you don't know about me. And I just don't feel we can go on with each other until I tell you.'"

Which, Andy told me, is exactly what she did. She didn't confess to being an ax murderer or a Russian spy, which is almost what Andy expected, given her solemn announcement. She simply talked about every lover she ever had. It wasn't even that there were that many. It's just that she went into such detail.

She began with her agonizing "first time," how much she had cared for Jim, how wonderful it was to discover herself sexually, how painful it was when they broke off. Then there was Peter, the commercial artist, the one who took her to fancy parties and introduced her to the most fascinating people she'd ever met. How romantic he was! ("What about me?" Andy kept asking himself.) And then Bob, the lawyer, and Jack . . .

The closer she came to the present, the more depressed Andy became. He kept trying to interrupt: "You really don't have to tell me all this"; but Margaret was a woman with a mission. Andy was confused and jealous. He'd had other lovers too. Was he supposed to tell Margaret all about them? Maybe she was still attracted to someone from before; maybe what she was really telling him was that he wasn't good enough.

Margaret ended her long litany with a deep breath. "I feel much better," she said a little uncertainly. "Don't you?"

Andy was by this time so driven into a shell that he didn't know what to say. One thing he didn't feel was better.

Nobody comes to a relationship without a past. We all have things we're proud of and not proud of; relationships which were wonderful, relationships which weren't. You bring your whole life to whatever new person you meet, and the other person does too. Margaret didn't intend to alienate Andy. She desperately wanted to let him in, and she felt the only way to do that was to lay everything on the table. But she fell into the trap of every person hellbent on being "honest." She didn't think of the effect all her confessions would have on Andy. She was honest without being attentive, sensitive, or kind. I'm happy to report Andy and Margaret recovered from her onslaught; he was finally able to tell her how hurt and confused he was by all of it. Margaret was genuinely surprised, until she imagined what it would have been like if Andy had confessed in the same way to her.

One reason we seem to revere blurting out the truth is that we hear it's good for us. Don't hold it in; spill it out; you'll feel better.

Carol Tavris, in her book *Anger: The Misunderstood Emotion*, questions this, and maybe we should too. Spilling out your guts doesn't always relieve stress, it often intensifies it. She cites the psychologist Thomas Gordon's differentiation between "I-messages" (saying what you feel simply to satisfy yourself, to "get it out") and "you-messages" (saying what you feel as an act of communication, talking to someone else).

The problem is that honesty for many of us has come to mean I-messages. We're bound by the myth that if we let it all out, we'll feel better. The fact is we rarely do, and the person with whom we're trying so hard to communicate is often left standing hurt and confused and farther away from us than before.

The frustrating thing about utter honesty is that we may have the best of intentions in trying to express it. Ann, a lovely and intelligent woman I know who teaches English at a small private school in Massachusetts, told me about just this frustration in an incident which happened to her during her first days at the school. The frustration, though, was not initially Ann's. Rather, it was that of a man who seemed bent on instant intimacy with her.

Ann is a slight, pretty woman in her early thirties. And shy. It took some courage for her to walk into the faculty lounge on a break after her first class, and introduce herself to her colleagues. The banter they so easily engaged in, the politics of the school she hadn't yet come to learn, all made it seem like a closed club. It was with some relief that she managed to engage the attention of another English teacher, Richard. Actually, "managed to engage" doesn't say it. Richard zoomed in on her like a jet plane onto a runway.

She was flattered at first, but some warning bell sounded as Richard spoke. For one thing, he'd barely said hello. "I'm very intuitive about people," he told her, "and for some reason I think we'll be able to talk. I've been watching you." (For how long? Ann wondered— she'd just walked into the room.) "And I can tell instantly that you've been through a lot. And it takes experience, doesn't it, to develop the deepest sensitivity. You've got it."

Ann was taken aback, and searched for something to say. "Well, I would like to get a rundown of things here, and it's awfully nice that you've offered to . . ."

Richard interrupted impatiently. He wasn't good at small talk, he said, especially not now. He'd just been through a painful divorce, and again, somehow, he "knew" that Ann would understand the pain. He made a dutiful apology about pouring all this out, but quickly went on to describe the frustrations he'd felt with his wife, how little she'd understood him. He talked nonstop for fifteen minutes.

"The thing is," Ann told me, "in some strange way I rather liked him. But it was overwhelming. Too much too soon. I even felt embarrassed. How could I greet him the next day? Talk about the weather?"

Ann was able to extract herself from Richard. Her next class was about to start and she fled the faculty lounge as if it were a prison. Later that day, when she had the time to reflect on Richard's outpouring, she felt a new emotion grow—anger. She realized all of Richard's questions were rhetorical; all of his "confession" was directed to nobody but himself. It was as if he hadn't been talking to her at all.

Richard may be an exaggerated example of how self-expression can be exactly that: expressing yourself to nobody but yourself. Ann, although angry at Richard, still felt for him. Running the tape of his deepest feelings on and on wasn't doing him any good. His honesty wasn't cleansing. It fed on itself and built a stronger wall around him than if he'd been able to keep it all inside.

There are subtler and far more effective ways to be honest than most people realize. What about the difficult times when something—even something superficial, like how a person dresses or eats—bothers you to such an extent that you feel you have to bring it up? The quintessential Victorian might advise you to grin and bear it. A seventies radical might tell you to come out with the truth as bluntly as you feel like telling it.

You don't have to do either.

One couple I interviewed discovered a much better solution. Tony is a second-generation Italian who comes from a large and close family—Mama stirring the pot, seven raucous kids vying for attention, and the authority figure, Papa, at the head of the table. Meals were events in Tony's childhood. Eating was a serious and lusty business. Not a whole lot of attention was paid to table manners. You ate as much as you could as fast as you could; you bartered for the best piece of meat or the largest piece of cake.

It was exactly his vitality which attracted Emily to Tony. He seemed more alive to her than any man she'd met. His background couldn't have been more different from her own. Emily came from a Midwestern middle-class home in which everything had its place, everything was orderly to a fault. She'd learned the right order of forks and spoons while setting the table, was careful to unfold her napkin and put it in her lap, and waited politely to pick up her fork only after her mother had done so. Dinner was a time when everyone conversed about the day's events in careful, modulated tones. And nobody chewed with his mouth open.

Emily happily fled most of those restrictions, and life with Tony was refreshing and unbridled. But Emily quickly realized that one vestige of her upbringing hadn't left her. By the time she and Tony were married for a year and a half, she was slowly driven crazy by the fact that Tony chewed with his mouth open. "I knew it was silly to be so bothered by it, but it became the only thing I could think about when we had dinner. It drove me up the wall! I got to a point where I'd make up excuses for having to leave the room—a phone call I absolutely had to make in the middle of dinner, for instance. Finally, when I was getting up often enough to attract Tony's attention, which isn't easy to do when he eats, he asked me if something was the matter." Emily had two choices, an I-message ("You eat like a pig!") or a you-message. She paused and chose the latter. She saw the innocence in his eyes. He really had no idea what was upsetting her.

She told Tony about a barbecue she'd been to when she was six, a big family occasion at her grandparents' house. They had her favorite food, chicken legs and corn on the cob. She remembered sitting at the long picnic table, the youngest child there, her relatives all around getting quieter and quieter as she happily tore into her food. Suddenly the silence was deafening. Little Emily looked up to see her parents glaring at her and her grandfather clearing his throat, looking the other way.

"Polite people do not eat with their mouths open," her father sternly informed her.

Emily was astonished. "How do they get the food in, then?"

Tony laughed. And then the point dawned on him. He looked a little astonished too. "*That's* what's been bothering you?"

"What's bothering me is *me*," Emily said. "For years afterwards, at every meal, I tried to eat like some weird robot, hardly moving my jaws." She said she became sensitive to and bothered by people who didn't try to do the same thing, even though she eventually realized how silly it was. "But it still bothers me," she told Tony gently. "One neurosis I haven't gotten rid of, I guess."

Tony sat up straight in his chair, carefully dabbed his lips with a napkin, took a sip of water with his little finger outstretched: a perfect parody of an English lord. Both of them burst out laughing.

But he ate a lot quieter thereafter.

How much worse this scenario might have been if Emily had chosen the less tactful approach! Relationships have broken up over less. Emily's expression of honesty took some time and planning and care. The reward was that it nurtured her relationship with Tony. She allowed the expression of her feelings to bring them together, not force them apart.

There are times when you can show too much caring, however. You may be, or have known, the kind of adoring lover whose beloved is the world to him, the kind of person who'll go to any length to express his adoration. Flowers, candy, wine, and candlelight are the least of it. Phone calls throughout the day to see how you are, gifts and letters at the least expected times; nothing is too great or small to express for the person who becomes obsessed with showing his affection.

And the thing is, he's perfectly sincere about it. He's merely being honest about his feelings.

Gail, a successful marketing executive and a very attractive woman in her mid-thirties, is someone I've known for many years, and there's little about what goes on between men and women that she can't illuminate.

Gail told me about a fiercely honest man with whom she'd been involved: Raoul.

"At first I thought it might have been a cultural difference. Raoul is Brazilian, and the kind of lavish attention he gave me I was ready to chalk up to some stereotyped 'Latin' love. But I slowly realized that his several phone calls a day, long-stemmed roses, and endless praise of me was simply who he was. None of it was a 'line.' He really meant all his protestations of love. It's just that there were too many of them."

The dates Gail had with Raoul quickly became excruciating for her. She felt trapped and, finally, bored. "He talked nonstop about what a goddess I was. I was intelligent; I was beautiful. He had never met a woman like me before. It would go on for hours. And the killer was his parting line: 'I really love talking with you.' *With me? I hadn't said a word!"*

Most of us go through times when we're so head-over-heels in love that we can't see straight. They can be wonderful, and we couldn't be more honest at these times. Every declaration of love feels like a statement of eternal truth.

What we don't realize is that the message may not be coming across. Not the way we'd like it to. Raoul and, often, the rest of us are so bound up in our own experience of love that we block out the very person who occasions that love. We don't take care to see what effect we're having. We may be terribly honest about our feelings, but to no avail. Slowly we find out that the person we most want to listen isn't listening.

The main message is this: there's a huge difference between knowing something and saying it. Strangely, saying everything you feel can distort the truth, not express it. Words can clamp down on a feeling, limiting it in ways you may not want to. Pinning down the wings of a butterfly prevents it from ever flying again; sometimes indiscriminately saying what you think can do the same thing.

What about anger? There are times we all see red, when walking on eggshells and taking the time and care to come up with just the right words strike us as impossible. What do you do then?

Being honest about the anger you feel can take a wide variety of forms. There's a great difference between justifiable anger and something that merely irks you. Justifiable anger, for the majority of us who lack Gandhi's demeanor, will sometimes require harsher expression. But again we come to a choice. Carol Tavris sums it up neatly: "For most of the small indignities of life, the best remedy is a Charlie Chaplin movie. For the larger indignities, fight back. And learn the difference."

When does honesty require fighting back in a love relationship?

One of the most difficult emotions people must deal with is jealousy. We've all at some time suffered real or imagined feelings of betrayal, when a lover does something you just can't fathom, something which hurts you deeply. What is the best way to be honest about these feelings?

The first step is to "learn the difference." Count to ten, or to whatever number will give you time to figure out if the betrayal is real or imagined. Stan, a friend of mine from law school, admits to being a "naturally" jealous person. He's possessive about the woman he's involved with, and often sees "betrayal" when it isn't there. Stan, though, learned to "check" himself before blurting out an accusation by adding a dose of reason to the pot. When he gives himself time to reflect, he usually realizes he's made the whole thing up. He used to "talk it out" by expressing the first feelings which struck him, and most of his relationships broke up as a result.

But some betrayals are real.

I received a poignant letter from a young woman in California describing a betrayal which was all too real:

> . . . when I realized that Tom was seeing another woman, my first feeling was to get back at him. I'd suspected something was going on, but tried to explain it away—his work wasn't going well, he'd just hit his thirty-fifth birthday which for some reason made him feel "middle-aged." But then I saw him downtown with the woman. He was letting her out of his car, and he kissed her goodbye. . . .

This woman wrote that she planned any number of ways she'd "get back" at her lover; she staged violent, dramatic scenes in her imagination. Nothing, though, could take away the hurt. No strategy seemed to make her feel better. What did she end up doing?

> . . . I simply let my heart speak. When he came home that night, I asked him to sit down. I took a deep breath and told him I knew what was going on and that he had hurt me more deeply than he would ever know. . . .

She could have thrown a lamp at him. Instead she told the truth. His reaction?

. . . It was as if I *had* thrown a lamp at him. He looked down at his feet, then into my eyes. He must have expected some kind of blowup, but something in me told me that wasn't the way to handle things. We finally decided to go out and take a walk. Not talk. Just a walk. I couldn't forgive him yet. I still felt the incredible pain. But at least we were together honestly, for the first time in so long.

The woman continued her letter, saying the wound still hadn't healed, but that they had reached a point where they could talk about their dissatisfactions, their fears, their mistakes. And slowly her desire for vengeance was replaced by the desire to understand him, and to have him understand her. They're still together, and they're growing closer.

Fighting back can mean telling the simple, unglossed truth. While the woman who wrote this letter didn't scream bloody murder at her lover, there *are* times when a good shouting match can clear the air more effectively than anything else. If you *care* about the person with whom you're angry, your honesty will have a cleansing effect and not a vicious, damaging one. Angry honesty can still be sensitive.

In fact, the bottom line is that honesty is truly effective *only* if it's expressed sensitively. The continual awareness that what you say to someone will have an effect—that any exchange between you involves both of you, and that you both have feelings which require respect—isn't an encumbering awareness. It's a freeing one.

Men and women are sometimes never more polarized than when they think they're being honest. Telling the truth is a delicate process, a process which is truly helpful or enlightening only when it involves both of you. Taking the time to look into your lover's eyes and heart before you speak is the only guarantee that your message will get across.

9

Love and Money

HAPPINESS, Freud tells us, depends on success in love and work. Whatever else you may think about Dr. Freud, I suspect you'll agree with him on this point. Love and work are the two key poles in our lives, and it seems to me that we define ourselves from the two bases they represent: who we are and what we do. Love, as we've already begun to see, helps to tell us who we are, and being satisfied in love—if it's true satisfaction—has to mean in some sense being satisfied with ourselves. As for what we "do"—well, in the U.S.A. in the twentieth century, we've generally let our jobs describe that for us. A common problem is that most of us attempt to wrest more happiness from our jobs than our jobs can give us. And we do this because we're told it's the only happiness we can count on.

We're not told it's never enough.

For the vast majority of men and an increasing number of women, work is the only activity they feel they can trust to give them satisfaction. The phenomenon of the "workaholic" is now widespread. Our bosses are surrogate parents, coworkers are siblings, offices are our homes. God forbid that we don't get that hoped-for promotion: that means corporate Daddy and Mommy don't approve of us. And worse is getting fired: we face the ultimate horror of being kicked out, disowned. Our whole sense of self-worth is bound up in the "success" of what we do, and by success we rarely mean more than a boss's or coworker's approval. Paychecks are gestures of that approval—the higher the amount, the greater the "love" we feel we've earned.

The problem with being married to a job is obvious: you may be able to take it home with you, but those unfinished reports due tomorrow and that muddle of anxiety and fear you take home in your head don't constitute a human being you can hold, comfort, be comforted by, understand, and make love to.

If Freud is right about needing a balance between work and love to be happy—and I think he is—we've got to correct the balance which, in most of our lives today, is lopsidedly in favor of work. There's a loneliness no job can fill. Our American work ethic may have many virtues, but it cannot take away the ache we feel for the complete satisfaction of romantic love.

The next time you're at any kind of social gathering, listen to how people introduce themselves—in fact, listen to how you introduce yourself. The first question after "What's your name?" is almost invariably "What do you do?" And then comes the résumé: "I'm vice-president of marketing at John Doe, Inc.," "I'm sales representative at . . . ," and so forth. Listen to the people who obviously don't feel their jobs (that is, they) are impressive enough. A secretary might cover up his or her supposedly lowly position with the catch phrase "administrative assistant"; the unemployed will describe themselves as "between jobs." The fear of not being thought impressive in work has approached paranoia.

And now listen to Sandra, a lovely young woman I met at a party not too long ago. I admit I'm not immune to asking the automatic question, "What do you do?" and I asked it of Sandra.

"You mean what did I do today?" she asked me. "Well, let's see—I got up at eight in the morning to bake bread, then I took my winter coats to be stored at the dry cleaners, then I called my friend Joe to see if he wanted to catch one of the Fellini films they're running at this month's retrospective downtown . . ." She paused for a moment and looked me in the eye to make sure I was questioning my own question. "Oh yes, then I practiced the flute. I just started taking lessons."

She smiled, and I got the point.

Sandra realized that what we "do" comprises far more than what we do to make a living. As it happens, she eventually got around to telling me about her work— which she thought of as an activity she enjoyed doing rather than a "job"—and I was treated to a fascinating description of the strange, funny customers she bumps into at a department store where she's a saleswoman. In fact, I was laughing so hard at one point that half the party looked in our direction to see what was going on. I found myself a lot more impressed by what Sandra "did" than I ever could have been listening to some top executive running down his list of achievements.

We've got to loosen the hold work has on us, not only because love and romance don't have a chance when work takes over, but because finding our self-worth in nothing but a job puts us in a dangerously precarious position. We are more than what we do. We are also how we love.

Ron, whom I once worked with at a law firm in New York City, lost a great deal more than he gained when he became so consumed with his job that he forgot how to love.

Ron was undoubtedly brilliant. He was the firm's superstar; he climbed the corporate ladder and became a partner faster than anyone else in the firm's history. He did what he knew was required to reach the rank he desired: twelve-hour days, weekend meetings with the "right" people, complete sensitization to the power shifts within the firm—his job was his life.

The problem was that Ron had another life that was totally neglected. He had been married to a lovely, gracious woman for ten years, and had two small children. They had recently bought a beautiful home on the sprawling acreage of Sands Point. Ron thought himself to be lucky beyond belief: great job, nice house, and a family. It was all he had worked for.

I ran into Ron in the firm's cafeteria late one night when we were both coming in for a last cup of coffee. I spoke to him about his latest, and biggest, promotion.

"Ron, I know it's supposed to be a secret but you know how news travels around this place—congratulations!"

Ron looked at me, gave me a wry smile, and then just shook his head and said, "Let me give you some advice."

We sat down and Ron continued.

"I may be a hell of a success story here but at home, well, that's a different story. My wife told me last week that it was over. I had no idea what she was talking about. She told me that making love to me was like making love to a law review. You know how hard I've worked here, Mike. And I thought she appreciated the things I was able to give her because of that work. She told me she didn't want 'things,' she wanted me."

I tried to console Ron and said, "I'm sure you two will work it out."

He bowed his head, stared at the floor, and very quietly said, "I don't think so. I'm going on a sabbatical for a few months to try to straighten myself out."

He looked up at me then and offered his advice.

"Work hard and work well, Mike, but slow down the process. It may take you five more years to get there—wherever 'there' is—but at least the rest of your life will be intact when you do."

Does Ron remind you of anyone you know? I think we have all met a Willy Loman or two, and there is probably more than a bit of Willy in most of us. But adhering fanatically to a job can't help but have a damaging effect on one's love life. I'm not saying that ambition is bad or that success in work doesn't have some very satisfying rewards which transcend money. But there's a half of yourself that suffers from neglect when the job becomes the end-all, and it is this part of your life that desperately cries out for attention.

When that half is neglected for an extended period of time, when work and love are in a state of imbalance, self-destructiveness seems to be right around the corner. I

don't know either Wayne Hayes or Wilbur Mills person-
ally, but I believe the sexual affairs that destroyed these
two powerful politicians were the result of exactly this
type of imbalance—a tragic imbalance.

We ought to think long and hard about our priorities.
If the job gets top billing, the relationship has to suffer.
Why not have an ongoing affair with your job? Make the
job the "other woman"; devote forty hours a week to
your affair, and don't always bring stories and problems
about your affair home with you.

It was common fodder for popular novels and situation comedies some years ago to picture a housewife neglected by her businessman husband—a man whose
work always seemed to keep him away. With women in
the work force in larger numbers than ever before, a more
and more common problem is the division that comes between two working lovers or spouses. More and more relationships are breaking up because of this divisive
setup—sometimes because a woman is expected to keep
the household in perfect order in addition to working full
time; sometimes the relationship fails simply because a
man and a woman discover that they like their jobs more
than they like each other. Dr. Philip Blumstein and Dr.
Pepper Schwartz in their 1983 study, *American Couples,*
tell us one hard truth they learned from hundreds of in-
terviews: without at least one "relationship-centered"
partner in a couple, the relationship is doomed to fail.
What this implies is that at least one person has to give
more than fifty percent of his or her time and attention to
love rather than to work. But is it possible for both lovers
to balance the two—to achieve both satisfactions? I've
painted a pretty bleak picture so far of how erosive work

can be to a relationship; how can work and love be integrated?

The first lesson is: stay in touch.

Remember that if you're part of a couple, you've made a commitment to another person that is as important as the obligation you've made to work. The welcome news is that these commitments don't have to bang heads. In fact, the presence—sometimes even the imagined presence—of a lover can help you in the midst of your most stressful times on the job.

Pete, a man in his mid-thirties who works as an engineer in the design department of a major automobile company, had this to say: "The pressures can mount up unbelievably. There seem to be fourteen deadlines around every corner. Sometimes, when every light on my phone is blinking at me, I motion to my secretary a sign she correctly translates as 'cool it for a minute.' I close my office door, take a deep breath, and sit back in my chair. I think of Loren, my wife. It's like I can almost bring her into the room. I imagine her coming up behind me and putting her cool hands on my forehead. I get this incredible sense of peace—she calms me down."

If he knows Loren can be reached—and often she can't, because she works in a nursing home, where she's usually with a patient and can't be disturbed—Pete will call her, just for the sound of her voice. But whether or not he can actually talk to her, Loren represents a kind of oasis for Pete—a loving presence he can turn to at the worst as well as the best of times.

And of course the best of times can present a happy occasion for a reunion with a lover too. Karen, a woman who lives in Boston and recently received a promotion from associate editor to editor at a publishing house, told me she learned this lesson in rather a roundabout way. Her boyfriend Richard works for a major insurance company also in Boston, and Karen often felt uneasy about telling him the details of her work in publishing—she was afraid that he wouldn't be interested. Their jobs seemed to be worlds apart. In fact, whenever they met and the conversation turned to work, she encouraged Richard to tell her about his; she told me she didn't want to bore him with hers. As a result, Richard didn't know a whole lot about what Karen did for a living—he just assumed that Karen wasn't very much interested in her job. Richard could not be faulted for not knowing that Karen in fact was passionate about the publishing business.

When Karen heard about her move up, however, she was bursting with the news. She felt she'd worked hard for the promotion, and she was excited by the possibilities it offered. On a quick impulse she dialed Richard at his office. He got on the line—but he sounded rushed, harassed. "Sorry, honey, it's wild today. Don't have time. Is it anything important?"

Karen felt self-conscious. "No, nothing."

"Well," the obviously harried Richard replied, "meet you tonight for dinner? It'll have to be later than usual— I'm tied up here 'til seven."

"Sure," Karen said. She decided her news wouldn't be that interesting to Richard after all.

They met later that night at a restaurant, and a half hour into their conversation, which as usual was Richard's recitation of crises at work, he remembered Karen's call that afternoon. "What did you want to tell me?"

"Oh, it's really nothing," Karen said, looking down at her plate. "Just something about work."

"What?" Karen was surprised at Richard's eager tone.

"I got a promotion," Karen said, looking up.

Richard beamed. "That's terrific! Tell me about it!"

Karen was amazed at his enthusiasm. She told Richard what the promotion was and, prodded by him, told him how much it meant to her. Encouraged by her boyfriend's genuine interest, Karen found herself spilling out all that she'd withheld from Richard. "But I never knew this!" Richard kept saying. He was more than genuinely interested—he loved seeing Karen glow as she went into more and more detail.

When you express interest in someone's work—genuine interest—you're saying more than that you're interested in this or that particular line of work. While I've said that work to the exclusion of all else can lead to emotional misery and a fragile sense of self-worth, what we spend forty hours a week doing is a part of us—and it can't help but absorb many of our concerns, dreams, and hopes. Karen felt Richard cared about her as much as he cared about what she was doing. An enormous part of herself, even an essential part, was now available to the man she loved most. Her work has become something important she can share with him.

Sadly, women are too often reluctant to share their job experiences with men—and the more successful they are, the greater the reluctance. I've heard many tales similar to Karen's—and I've known many women who've been automatically reluctant to discuss their own successes because they fear their accomplishments are some-how potentially emasculating. "What man wants a woman who is successful in work?" they think. And what if, heaven forbid, it turns out she makes more money than he?

The key to talking about your work romantically is talking about it honestly, whether you're a woman or a man. Take the cue from Sandra, the woman I met who made her sales job sound as fascinating as any career I've heard of. She made it sound fascinating because her job really was fascinating to her. But Sandra did more than that. Rather than giving me a laundry-list description of her duties, or a pumped-up, self-congratulatory collection of success stories, she talked about her work in a way that engaged me because of her honest enthusiasm. Work is finally no less "human" an activity than love, and making a connection between the two in your own life means you can share both work and love with someone in a way that attracts rather than repels.

Finally, set your priorities so that they reflect what you want, not what you think is expected of you. One young woman I know who just turned thirty had to make some hard decisions about the role of work in her life. Although she has just received her license as a stock-broker, she has also just gotten married. While some women's magazines exhort her to become a superwife, and later a supermom, she finally decided that at this point in her life her marriage was more important than her career. She also wants children and does not want to have to assign them to years of day care while she pur-sues a career. She realized that to be successful in her career as a stockbroker she would have to put in many more hours than forty a week—and she finally decided she just wasn't prepared to do that. "I'm not being lazy," she said. "I'm being sensible."

There are no easy answers when, out of economic necessity, both the man and the woman have to work long hours. But I know a number of dual-career couples who manage, in large part because they are able to keep a sense of humor—which also means they've cultivated a healthy perspective about work.

Gary and Joan are one such a couple. They not only call each other when they can during the day, they also make time for lunch when they can. Both respect the pressures they have to contend with at their equally de-manding jobs: coming home at the end of the day is for both of them a welcome, loving, and joyful reunion.

And, every so often, something happens that causes both of them to make a decision that shows just who's "boss" in their lives. Here is a delightful example.

Gary is a postal inspector at a busy branch of the U.S. Post Office in Washington, D.C. Joan is equally harried as a legal secretary. Gary grabbed a cup of coffee at four o'clock one afternoon and paused to call Joan.

"I'm going wacko!" Joan muttered into the phone when she heard Gary's voice. "If I were three people I couldn't get all this stuff done."

"Hey, honey, the day's almost over . . ." Joan never heard the last words because she had to put Gary on hold to take care of an incoming call.

After a moment she clicked back on. "You'll never believe the jerk who just . . ." she said, putting Gary on hold once again—there was another incoming call.

"Honey?" Gary thought he heard the click of Joan

coming on again, which she may have done for a second, but he was again put on hold. Joan wasn't kidding about being busy.

Gary decided there was no point in hanging on—this was obviously one of those days for her. His hadn't exactly been a bed of roses either. Suddenly he got a slightly wicked gleam in his eye. "Hey, Joe!" he called over to a coworker. "Cover for me, okay? Got an emergency." Joe nodded that that was okay, and Gary grabbed his coat and closed it tight—it was a bitter January in Washington—and sneaked out the back door.

He arrived at 4:45 at Joan's office, fifteen minutes before the end of her day. Joan looked up at him, astonished, a phone at each ear. Just that moment her boss, Mr. Newton, walked out of his office. He turned automatically to Joan to give her an instruction, when he felt the tap of a mittened hand on his back.

"I'm sorry, Mr. Newton, but I'm Joan's husband and there has been an emergency," Gary said in his gravest tone. "She's got to get home immediately."

Mr. Newton looked at him with concern. "Well, of course," he said. Gary wore a very convincing somber face. "Will everything be all right?"

Gary nodded. "As long as I can get her home quickly," he said.

Joan was staring, wide-mouthed and in shock, at her husband. "What's—?" she managed to say, until she caught Gary's wink.

"It's not Aunt Martha, is it?" Joan said in mock horror, playing along.

"I'm afraid it is, honey." Gary was awfully good at this.

Mr. Newton let her go with his blessings.

Bundled in their coats and looking like the picture of propriety, Joan and Gary walked quickly out of the office. When they were a safe block away, both let out a whoop of laughter. "You were terrific!" Joan shouted, hugging her husband wildly. "Why didn't you come sooner?!" But Gary gave her that wicked gleam again and they piled into their car, which was parked around the corner. It began to snow, first lightly, then heavily enough to dust the windshield thickly, and soon, while they huddled together in the front seat, the snow blanketed the car completely. Joan nuzzled Gary warmly.

"How does it feel to be kidnapped?" Gary asked.

"Wonderful," Joan whispered, before she kissed him.

Now, before we go any further: I'm *not* telling you to walk out on your bosses. I'm only telling you that your life is your own, and that sometimes—at least fifty percent of the time, in fact—you might want to consider sharing that life with the human being who loves you best in the world. That human being is rarely your boss.

10

Being Together and Apart

"**D**O YOUR OWN THING"; "I'm okay, you're okay"; "I need more space"; "the 'me' generation": according to these popular phrases, independence should be the ultimate goal in modern-day life, even for couples in love. Hipness means not caring; "cool" is a sign of strength. A confession that you long for companionship or yearn for more of someone's time could be a white flag that tells the world, "I am weak."

This myth, which many seem to embrace, makes for a lot of very unhappy people. We've got to learn that, while you're okay and I'm okay, it's also okay to say "I miss you."

Expressing your feelings always is put to the test when you face particularly long separations from your lover: a business trip, maybe, or a trip to visit the family. Even the daily separation of going to work can put pressure on a relationship. A woman may wonder what her husband is really up to when he calls to say, "Don't wait up, I'll be late." The husband may wonder if his wife actually has a sick aunt who needs her immediate—and sole—attention. But we rarely dare to make a big deal out of it. We can't appear to "miss" each other too strongly. We don't, after all, want to appear weak.

Being apart doesn't have to produce these tensions. In fact, you can transform the inevitable, temporary separations from your lover into an opportunity to heighten romance. One of the greatest romantic joys in life is to reunite. Letting your lover know you miss him and being overjoyed when he returns aren't admissions of weakness. Those emotions can make you closer than ever before, although some couples, like Joan and Don, have learned this the hard way.

They met at an antinuclear rally in Washington, D.C. The exhilaration of being part of a committed group reminded both of them of the anti–Vietnam War demonstrations during their college years. They felt attracted to one another physically as well as politically. Both felt a sense of exhilaration and liberation, and they also felt free from society's conventions and prejudices. "Alternate lifestyle" is a phrase they might have invented: Don was the editor of a national labor newsletter; Joan worked with emotionally disturbed and underprivileged children, and when they decided to move in with each other, each was adamant about having a "no-strings-attached relationship." Jealousy was out of the question—it represented a kind of archaic morality. "Together" people don't cling, they agreed. Don's work occasionally took him to meetings and conventions around the country; Joan, tied to work at her clinic, could rarely accompany him. But that was fine: "I mean, we weren't married or anything," she said.

There were so few strings, in fact, that Don seldom announced he was leaving when he had to take a trip. He simply left. Sometimes he put a note on the refrigerator door with a cryptic message ("Gone for the week, see you"). But often he didn't even make that effort. Gradually Joan became astonished—and embarrassed—that his unannounced entrances and exits bothered her, considering their open relationship.

"It would especially hit me when I would come home with something really terrific to tell Don," Joan confessed, "like when some kid diagnosed as autistic said 'hi' to me. Don just wouldn't be there. I felt like something had been yanked out of me—I felt terribly alone. But what made it even worse is that I wasn't supposed to feel this way. Don and I had no obligations to each other—that wasn't in the script."

When Don reappeared as unexpectedly as he left, Joan was careful to hide her feelings. A nonchalant "hi" was the greeting she felt he expected.

"Things got really bad," she continued. "He began to get moody, which he had never been before. And though I couldn't believe it, I began to suspect that he was seeing other women. And I hated myself for imagining it, because, again, I wasn't supposed to care. Then something surprising happened."

Don walked into their apartment after work one day and slammed a pile of manuscripts onto the kitchen table. Joan was amazed at this unusual display of emotion. He was really angry. "Look," he said to her, not meeting her eyes, "I don't know quite how to say this, but . . ." (Joan froze, expecting her fears about "another woman" to be confirmed.) He cleared his throat and said in a barely audible mumble, "How come you never seem glad to see me?"

You could have knocked Joan over with the proverbial feather.

"I was incredibly touched," she told me, "but I still didn't feel I could express it. We had never talked about our feelings for one another before. Almost instinctively, I became angry too."

"Well, how come you come and go without telling me anything?" she spat back at him.

"Because I didn't think that you gave a damn!"

"Well, I didn't think that *you* gave a damn!"

"Well, I do!" The shouting match continued.

"Yeah? Well, I do too!" came the equally enraged response.

They stood toe to toe telling each other they loved each other in the only way they knew how.

"It was wonderful," Joan recalled, smiling. "Here we were screaming that we cared about one another, after so many months of screaming the same things silently inside." Finally, after their "fight," they both broke into laughter.

Leave-takings can be dramatic little events. The way you show your sorrow when your lover leaves and your delight at his return can make both moments rich and romantic. The woman who makes it clear that she will miss her lover when he leaves on a trip really is telling him something far more important: her love for him matters—matters a lot. And knowing you're missed becomes a precious gift that you carry with you. You are never really apart when you know someone is thinking of you.

I know another couple who occasionally are separated for as long as two weeks at a time, although they would prefer to spend their time together. The "gifts" they give each other, however, make any separation just one more indication of how much they love each other.

Mary is a woman from a strongly principled, strict Midwestern background. But despite the rigor of her upbringing, she's got a wonderful, childlike sense of humor and the ability to please and feel pleased. She enjoys poking a little fun at her husband, Jim, who comes from a similarly "proper" background, although he isn't nearly as spontaneous as she is. Jim, ostensibly disapproving of Mary's whimsical attentions, loves every minute of it. He gave me one example.

"The notes! It must have been in the middle of the night before she had to leave on a business trip to Milwaukee that Mary snuck all around the house and attached little yellow notes in various unexpected places. You know, the little pieces of paper with the adhesive on one end? She went to a lot of trouble."

The next morning, while driving home from the airport, after he and Mary had said their goodbyes, Jim found the first of her notes when he pulled down the sun visor in his car. (He hadn't even gotten out of the airport parking lot.) The note simply said, "Miss me yet?"—and Jim's only thought at the moment was a definite yes. He glanced to his right and saw another square of yellow, affixed to the passengaer seat: "Wish I were here." Later, when Jim arrived home, he found more of the notes. Mary had thought out what each of Jim's activities would be in her absence and planted each note accordingly. So, when he lifted the lid off a container of stew she had prepared and frozen for him, he found yet another little yellow square, which read: "If love be the food of God, hope you like beef stew." (He's still trying to figure out what that one meant.)

There were more notes, Jim said, but the last one perhaps was the least expected. As he went to pour himself an after-dinner drink before retiring for the night, Jim opened a bottle of his favorite brandy, only to find yet another of the telltale yellow notes, stuck to the bottom of the bottle! "Pining away and drowning your sorrows?" the note on the bottle read. "Don't worry, I'll be calling you in an hour." (Which she did, knowing exactly when he'd be done reading the paper but still be awake.)

Some might think Mary may have gone a little overboard, but she knew what seemingly silly things would please her husband. A glance at the refrigerator in their house during one of Mary's trips would be proof enough that Jim was certainly pleased. He stuck all the notes he had found up and down the refrigerator door and proudly pointed them out to anyone who came over— from the plumber to his boss.

So far we've heard from couples who didn't want to be apart but who learned how to express their feelings in unmistakably romantic ways. Sometimes, however, a couple *should* temporarily separate; different kinds of absences sometimes can make the heart grow fonder.

A friend of mine, Ruth, says she needs time apart from her lover. "It's like my time to recharge," she said. "I call it my quiet time." Ruth said that sometimes she takes a long, peaceful drive in the country; sometimes she simply curls up with a good book. "My boyfriend always sees the difference in me when I return. He says I 'glow'! I don't know if I glow or not," she added, "but I sure feel better. And I feel I have so much more to give him after one of my mini-vacations. I feel calmer, more loving." Another dividend: "He also knows that when I am with him I want to be with him. I'm not there out of habit."

You probably know that all lovers are not as understanding as Ruth's boyfriend about voluntary absences. There are times when you have to explain very carefully that your occasional need to be alone isn't a rebuff or an excuse to get away because you don't like being with someone. The key is to be honest about it. Never assume your lover magically understands your need for privacy. Always reassure your lover that the private time you're taking isn't only for you—it will help both of you.

Can one lover's private time—however well intentioned—be overdone? Theoretically, we should all be able to take whatever time we need, but if you're not sensitive to the effect you're having on your neglected partner, you may find yourself with more private time than you bargained for. The relationship between Jennifer and her tennis-playing husband, Steve, nearly came to a standstill because of simple neglect. Steve is the kind of tennis nut who is completely filled with the game—his weekends were almost completely filled with tennis matches. Jennifer, who is neither athletic nor interested in tennis, completely understood that Steve felt terrific after playing—that her husband needed tennis to be happy. But she couldn't help but feel that the time he spent away from her was excessive. Quite frankly, she was lonely.

"I didn't even bother suggesting that we do something together on the weekends," Jennifer told me. "I just accepted the fact that Steve 'needed' his tennis. But then I started to get annoyed—wasn't I entitled to some time with him too? We both work during the week, and we simply didn't spend any time with one another."

Finally Jennifer confronted Steve, who was truly oblivious to the fact that his tennis obsession was bothering Jennifer ("I couldn't get mad at him," Jennifer said; "he really had no idea he was upsetting me"). Once Steve understood how much time he really was spending on the courts (he checked his tennis appointment book!), he couldn't blame Jennifer for being upset. Steve agreed to cut back on his tennis, and the two began to go on outings they enjoyed together.

"I was grateful to her," Steve said. "What if she hadn't said anything and just filed for divorce!"

Don't think that can't happen. Couples break up for what may seem to an outsider awfully trivial reasons. But nothing is trivial in an intimate relationship. It wasn't just tennis at stake here—it was the repeated absence of a lover missed and needed by his mate. Steve and Jennifer effected an easy reconciliation because they took the trouble to talk to one another, to listen and understand.

Some reconciliations aren't so easy. There are times when being apart for too long can cause serious damage. Temporary separations can also represent a prelude to something more final. There are times when nothing else can save a relationship—or end it more kindly—than separation. Jack and Roz are a couple in their early forties who had been married for twenty years. Slowly they came to realize that they were growing farther and farther apart. "Some of it," said Roz, "was simply that we weren't interested in the same things. When we were younger, that didn't matter much. When you're first starting out you're so much in love that nothing is an obstacle. But it became clearer and clearer, first to me, then to Jack, that we've spent years going in different directions. One morning we woke up and realized it."

Jack and Roz are in fact two very different personalities. Jack is a very successful computer consultant who keeps up with every new development in high technology—he's got a mind for detail and logic which Roz first found awesome, then found tiresome and boring. A successful woman herself, Roz devoted her time to a very different pursuit—she's a concert pianist. Her approach not only to music but to life was far more intuitive than Jack's. When she'd attempt to explain the emotional impact of a Chopin prelude to Jack, he'd draw a blank. Finally, Roz gave up and stopped talking to Jack about her work.

"I was just as unresponsive to him," she admitted. "He'd go into the most technical detail about this or that computer, so that I hadn't a hope of understanding. And frankly, I didn't have much desire to."

On that fateful morning, Roz made it clear for the first time in their marriage that she wasn't happy. Jack, normally uncomfortable with any demonstration of emotion, surprised Roz by agreeing with her: he wasn't happy either. They decided on a trial separation. Jack was able to move into a company apartment; Roz stayed on in their house.

Roz admitted that the first days of their separation were something of a relief to her. She could devote herself totally to her music, without feeling that she always was in the presence of someone who "couldn't understand." But then something a little strange happened.

"I was practicing some very complicated Bach and I became aware—really for the first time—of how intricately and mathematically the notes fit together. I saw the math in the music! And instantly I thought of Jack. 'So this is what he's into,' I thought." Suddenly she felt lonely—she really missed him. She realized they'd never given each other a real chance to understand how their minds work. The spontaneous connection she made playing Bach opened up a whole new way of thinking about her husband.

"I called him that night, and asked if we could meet for dinner. He seemed more eager than I'd expected." Jack, as it turned out, was lonely too. And although he hadn't made a similar "intellectual" connection, Roz found him incredibly responsive to the insight she'd had about Bach. In fact (Roz said he was almost like a kid), he suggested making a graph of the mathematics in the piece. "We lay on the living room floor with paper and pen and we mapped out the piece," Roz said. "We felt like two kids with crayons and a coloring book!"

They talked long into the night. Jack began to open up about the excitement he felt in his work in a way Roz could completely understand. He, too, was "intuitive"; he could almost sense what was wrong with a computer when it needed to be fixed; he felt a kind of ESP about programs. Suddenly, Jack's work wasn't some impenetrable maze of detail and jargon to Roz—it was as "human" an activity as music. And music wasn't some imprecise "artistic" process to Jack—it had a real form and structure that fascinated him.

Suddenly they realized it was past midnight. Both were glowing with the discoveries they'd made about each other. Roz said Jack got up to leave. "Don't go" was all she said. And he didn't.

Jack and Roz's story is appealing to me for more than the obvious reason that they were able to be reconciled. There's something in the very dichotomy of their interests which symbolizes what romance is all about: it's the tension between intricate form and heartfelt feeling. What they discovered about each other wasn't only that their lines of work converged to a greater degree than they'd realized, but that their hearts and approaches to life did too. And a separation which might have led them to divorce instead gave them time to make that realization. You sometimes have to be deprived of love to realize how much you love or even *that* you do love.

One woman I know is perhaps more qualified to talk about what "being apart" can do to and for a relationship than almost anyone else I've talked to. Natalie lives five hundred miles from her boyfriend. He's in graduate school for one more year; she's locked into her job, and their main means of communication is the telephone. But they're more than holding out, as evidenced by one particular poem he sent Natalie not long ago, a short piece of verse by Hugh Prather. It's Natalie's favorite:

> Love, the magician,
> Knows this little trick
> Whereby two people walk
> In different directions
> Yet always remain
> Side by side

With all of this talk about being apart, isn't it permissible to travel together? Answer: whenever possible!

We'll touch on traveling together in a variety of other contexts, but here's one suggestion I'll leave you with here. Do it as often and imaginatively as possible. "Imaginatively" doesn't mean you have to find some undiscovered island in the Pacific and fly there by chartered plane. Sometimes, as Dorothy said, you'll find it a lot closer to your own backyard. One New York couple I know go to Philadelphia—an inexpensive hour and a half away—on the spur of the moment. He'll call her up in the middle of a Friday afternoon at work: "Wanna go?" She'll say, "Sure!" and by the early evening they'll be on a perfectly ordinary train bound for a perfectly ordinary motel for a perfectly extraordinary romantic weekend.

Get away together when you can; get away alone if you have to. But remember that both can—and should— be occasions for romance.

11

Hooray for Hollywood

THE HOLLYWOOD MOVIE is arguably the greatest cultural contribution this country has given the world. And up until the early 1970s, American movies were the greatest romantic teachers we've ever had or could hope for. Just remembering a few titles is enough to make my point: *Gone with the Wind, From Here to Eternity, Casablanca, Love in the Afternoon, Intermezzo.* Hollywood in the thirties, forties, and fifties gave us icons of romance which last to this day. Even if you're not an expert on the movies of Clark Gable, Marlon Brando, Marilyn Monroe, and any number of other screen legends, their names undoubtedly conjure up mythical images—a storybook time when men were handsome and brave, women adoring and beautiful. If romance began in the eleventh and twelfth centuries with ladies and their knights, surely its fulfillment found a face and a voice in Hollywood centuries later.

Then came Woody Allen.

Now, I've got nothing against Mr. Allen—he's a funny man and movies like *Manhattan* and *Annie Hall* undoubtedly reflect the angst and psychosexual mores of the decade and a half we've just survived. But put him in a duel with Errol Flynn? No contest.

Woody Allen represents a standard of "wimphood" which for a while even started to seem romantic—I remember reading (incredulously) lists of men whom women found "most attractive" in 1970s magazines, and there was Woody, right up there (well, almost) with Burt and Clint. But if my antennae are serving me correctly, we've all grown a little tired of the standard of "sensitivity"—and self-absorption—Woody Allen has been so successful in portraying.

Blair Sabol wrote (controversially) in a recent *Gentlemen's Quarterly* piece:

> It's now reached plague proportions. It's gone way beyond the mere quiche-eating epidemic. I'm talking about the number of men who are quickly falling under the spell of "wimp wonderment"—an overdose of warmth, sensitivity, vulnerability and supportiveness. And let me tell you, all this male niceness is plain nauseating. Suddenly I crave James Cagney to squeeze a grapefruit in my face.

And later:

> Believe me, at first Alan Alda's aura was a dream come true. Now the likes of him reek of marshmallow mundaneness. Too many men have simply become the sappiest side of their mothers.

I already anticipate the rotten eggs and tomatoes you

may be getting ready to throw at me, but although Ms. Sabol's words may be capable of inciting a riot, she's pointing out a real truth. A lot of women I've talked to are beginning to find the New, Open Man a pain in the neck.

You don't have to be a sociologist to realize that movies reflect the times they were made in—they're very reliable social barometers. Fred Astaire in top hat and tails, Ginger Rogers in chiffon and fur, reached an incredible peak of popularity smack in the middle of the Depression. People who could barely pay the rent flocked to see this magical and quintessentially romantic couple— if only to believe for an hour or two that romance and luxury and dancing did still exist—somewhere. Girls turned into clones of Jean Harlow, Joan Crawford, Garbo, Veronica Lake—whoever was the prevailing exemplar of female beauty at the time—and the men they dreamed of didn't know how to boil water, much less bake a quiche. A bunch of primitive sexists, huh?

But look what's happening today, smack in the middle of the 1980s.

Clint Eastwood. Burt Reynolds. Richard Gere. And a whole new generation of romantic young actors—Tom Cruise, Sean Penn, Lorenzo Lamas, among scores of others. Are women—and Hollywood—trying to tell us something?

A new generation of women actresses also bears out the trend to a New Romantic society—Debra Winger (whom Richard Gere ravished in *An Officer and a Gentleman* with almost the aplomb that Gable used with Leigh in *Gone With the Wind*) and the mostly mute but surpassingly sexy Daryl Hannah as the mermaid every man wants in *Splash*, to name only two.

Nobody seems to want to look—or act—like Diane Keaton anymore.

I said before that movies reflect their eras, and current movies are no exception. I'm not saying that we've suddenly recovered the magical, romantic aura of the 1930s Hollywood movie; movies such as *Tootsie* and *Victor/Victoria* are enough to show that a fair amount of confusion remains in the air. But Clint and Burt continue to reign, and there's a reason.

Suzanne, a friend of mine and a woman who, at twenty-five, could not be expected to know much about Garbo, Bacall, Gable, or Grant firsthand (or even second), nonetheless described the effect Clint Eastwood had on her in a way that wouldn't be unusual in a twenty-five-year-old woman of 1942 describing Gary Cooper: "He doesn't have to say anything. He shows his emotions and feelings with his eyes, his actions. He's not the kind of guy to wear his heart on his sleeve, and I find that incredibly appealing." Clint Eastwood spoke succinctly for himself in an interview he once had with Norman Mailer: he said he'd finally arrived at the point in his career where he had "enough nerve to do and say nothing."

Burt Reynolds in his *Smokey and the Bandit* movies, Richard Gere in *American Gigolo* and *An Officer and a Gentleman*, and John Travolta in *Saturday Night Fever* give similar messages: they've got enough nerve—and self-confidence—to be the men who they know they are. No fuss, and few words. It's not hard to see their debt to Wayne and Brando.

By now I've either got you fuming or nodding (silently) in agreement. But what am I saying here? Men should start pushing grapefruit into their lovers' faces?

Of course not. But the fantasy that Hollywood has again begun to represent tells us a few clear truths. Remember that I'm calling for a romantic division of men and women, not a strict adherence to cave-man and cave-woman stereotypes.

I think we've had a little too much "realism." The trend back to the classic, romantic, and passionate love story, which I don't think has begun to peak in present-day Hollywood, isn't the only indication that we don't want an excess of "realism" pushed into our faces. In a piece entitled "The Return of Enchantment," which appeared in the *New York Times Magazine* (November 27, 1983), the cultural historian Kathleen Agena noted that "for many decades, a world of enchantment, of mystical beliefs and symbols, has been lurking in the shadows of our secular, advanced-technology culture. Now it has burst into the mainstream." Ms. Agena is talking about the proliferation of science fiction movies and books—*E.T.*, *Return of the Jedi*, *Superman I, II, III*, and so forth—which, she said is "startling." Our current society has a "fascination with mystical symbols and motifs that hark back to notions of an enchanted universe. . . ."

Kathleen Agena finds much to worry about in this particular return to enchantment, but the point I'm making here is that the need for fantasy, the need for "mystical beliefs and symbols," is one which pervades our romantic lives as well, and far from seeing it as a dangerous need, I think it's cause for celebration. A sense of enchantment is exactly what we've lacked in our love relationships, and anything which heightens that sense will necessarily heighten the pleasure we take in one another.

Hollywood movies can show us how to add enchantment to our lives, and not only in the imagination.

In a very funny article which appeared in *Vogue* (March 1984), Cynthia Heimel went as far as aping the speech and mannerisms of her favorite movie actress— Myrna Loy. This is perhaps farther than you'll want to go, but it makes a point:

> . . . modern movie stars will get you nowhere, role model-wise. I can't think of one of them who has wit, moral integrity and terrific outfits. One must stick with the old girls, who knew what was what. . . . I personally stick with Myrna. She's got the lightest touch. Who else could play poker with the boys in the baggage car and never remove her hat?

Cynthia Heimel then recounts an episode with her boyfriend: he "became furiously impatient with my fear of climbing a (small) mountain in the dark and left me alone on some wet rocks while he went exploring. . . ." Although her first impulse was to "sniffle a lot" when the "thoughtless cad" returned, she held onto her composure and, during the car ride home, imagined what Myrna Loy might have done in the same situation. When they finally got home, she turned to him and in her best Loyish accent announced, "Darling, you are an inconsiderate brat . . . Next time the climbing lust overtakes you, warn me first so I can take in a nice, warm movie instead of sitting around like a fool on wet rocks . . ." To his "But, but . . ." she replied, "Don't but me, you twit!" She continued "silkily": "I simply will not have it, and that's that." The next morning "he apologized prettily, I accepted him happily, and we were in perfect accord as I slipped into my satin dressing gown to go down for breakfast. Myrna would have been proud."

Cynthia Heimel obviously had fun with her impersonation—but the important point is her boyfriend did too!

You may be uncomfortable about staging a whole scene from a movie—but I'm not suggesting doing anything so artificial. The key, as I've said elsewhere, is to develop a romantic attitude, and Hollywood is a rich—close to infinite—source of clues of how to do that.

There's nothing wrong with playing roles.

Again we move into delicate territory. Most people are understandably reluctant to reveal the more imaginative romantic scenes they stage—or want to stage—with their lovers. It's too intimate a revelation, and the surest way to ruin fantasy is to have it laughed at. Of course, if you haven't explained to your lover that you've got a Tarzan-and-Jane fantasy before you start leaping from table to chair to sofa, you may have to resign yourself to exactly that response, but most fantasies—romantic fantasies—aren't quite so hazardous, even if they're exactly the same amount of fun. And fun, with Hollywood as our guide, is exactly what fantasy should be about!

One woman I talked to, Betty, a blond twenty-eight-year-old receptionist in a law office, revealed—a little nervously ("you promise you'll change my name in the book?")—a favorite fantasy she enacted with her lover, Daniel. It was her idea, she said, and it came to her when, on a Saturday afternoon window-shopping stroll, she happened to pass a "nostalgic" secondhand clothing store. In the window was a beaded, fringed, low-cut red satin dress—it looked like it could have been from the 1920s. Suddenly a vision of Marilyn Monroe, singing "That Old Black Magic" in her sweet come-hither voice, popped into Betty's mind. "I just smiled at the thought," Betty said. "That dress was exactly what Marilyn Monroe might have worn in a movie—and I started humming the tune as I continued to walk down the block. Slowly, as the song went through my head, and Marilyn's hips swayed to the rhythm of it, Marilyn became me! I'd never had the nerve to wear anything so outrageous, but I could really see myself in that dress! And when I began to imagine how Daniel might react . . ." She retraced her steps and bought the dress.

Several days later Daniel came to her apartment. She'd invited him for dinner. She'd staged the event carefully in her imagination. When he rang the bell, she let him in, her hair up in a kerchief, wearing sweat shirt and jeans—her usual weekend garb. Daniel kissed her somewhat dutifully and asked what was for dinner. "I told him he'd find out soon enough," said Betty, who then excused herself—she hadn't had time to change into "more comfortable" clothes. Before going into her bedroom to change, she put a record on the stereo—a twenty-five-year-old rendition of Marilyn Monroe's greatest hits. "What a great old recording!" was Daniel's half-interested comment. Betty lowered the lights before opening her bedroom door.

When she emerged—slowly, seductively—in the glittering red satin, Daniel's eyes turned into saucers.

Betty declined to go into the subsequent details of their evening (she cleared her throat and smiled at me), except to say that during one part of it Daniel did the most terrific imitation of Yves Montand in the movie *Let's Make Love*—complete with French accent—she could ever have imagined.

Let's face it. The problem with most fantasies—especially of the Hollywood variety—is that they read corny. But so powerful are our romantic connections to the great film love stories, they don't feel corny when you bring some aspect of them to life. Betty and Daniel played with each other in playing Screen Lovers—and under cover of their game were more intimate, passionate, and vulnerable than they could remember ever being before.

One couple who wrote to me were particularly imaginative about role-playing. In fact, their "Hollywood Romance Game" is the best one I've heard. It started out as exactly that—a game meant to make them laugh—and it's turned into something much more interesting. According to Jay, a thirty-year-old accountant (proof that accountants have received a lot of unwarranted bad press about their lack of imagination!), he suggested the idea to his lover, Carol. "I gave her six pieces of paper and a pen, and told her to write down the names of six Hollywood stars from the past or present she found the most attractive. Then I did the same. We put each of our sets of cards face down on either side of a table, and then shuffled each other's set, picking one at random to start with." The first name Jay picked was Cary Grant. Carol picked Sophia Loren. "We were pretty lucky," Jay wrote me. "They'd actually done a movie together, which we'd seen." They then acted out a love scene as the characters they'd picked.

Later in the evening, things got pretty interesting when Richard Gere met Jean Harlow! Sure, they laughed, sometimes in astonishment ("I didn't know you liked her!" Carol said when Jay's card said "Mia Farrow"), but eventually they found themselves in some very romantic "scenes." "It's fun, sexy, and I can't think of anything more romantic. I felt I'd met every woman I'd ever wanted to meet and all of them were Carol!"

Again, it may sound silly (and there was a time, Jay wrote, when E.T. met Zsa Zsa Gabor), but the fun and the imagination of the game led to some wonderful, romantic evenings. The childlike quality of sharing a fantasy—Hollywood or not—is always nurturing in a love relationship. When you accept your lover in his or her most outrageous guise, you've accepted your lover completely.

But the most interesting thing about playing out Hollywood roles is that it gives a man and a woman the chance to play openly the icons they've always secretly emulated and envied. A man can become, in Hollywood's terms, "a real man"; a woman can be whatever film heroine she may have always admired. Sure, it's a game, but I can't think of a more romantic one. And the best part about it is everybody wins!

12

Romantic Secrets from Around the World

THIS PAST New Year's Eve and New Year's Day I was invited to two parties. Both parties were traditional, family-oriented events, but the two could not have been more different.

The first party was given by my best friend, Arnold, and his wife, Janet. Arnold's roots go back to the Caribbean area; he and his family have spent many years living and traveling there.

Arnold exhibits all the outward signs of affection that we normally associate with southern Europeans and Latins. He greets with hugs and kisses. There is a great deal of physical closeness and constant touching. I watched Arnold tell a story to a group of people at his party; Janet was standing nearby. As Arnold explained his latest theories about everything from child rearing to roll-over mortgages, he moved closer to Janet, until he was resting one hand on her shoulder while gesturing constantly with the other. I could not only sense the chemistry between Janet and Arnold, I could see it. Not sexual, but a constant touching; a reminder, "I may be talking to a group of friends, but I want you to *know* that I'm also thinking about you."

The next day, I was invited by Sachiko to celebrate Oshoo Gatsu, the Japanese celebration of the New Year, at the home of her parents. Sachiko is Japanese and first-generation American, meaning that both her parents were born in Japan. Besides our eating sushi instead of steak and drinking sake instead of champagne, the difference between Arthur's party and Sachiko's was dramatic.

At one point during the party, Sachiko and I were talking to another couple, and I put my arm around her waist as we chatted. I don't consider myself overly demonstrative, so I was surprised when Sachiko's mother pulled me aside and told me that Sachiko's great-grandfather was a samurai, of the ancient warrior aristocracy of Japan, which followed a very strict code of chivalry called Bushido. She pointed out that the ultimate way in which a samurai could show his love for a woman was not to express it or show it. I got her point!

Sachiko later explained the Japanese way to me further. To the Japanese, most displays of overt affection or any type of spontaneous emotion show a weakness in devotion. All of the love one feels for another is expressed indirectly—that is, by focusing on rituals and routines that appear to the American eye to have nothing to do with romance or intimacy.

I, as well as most Americans, foster an inherent fascination with people who have lived, traveled, or were born abroad, and after my New Year's parties, I saw clearly why we should be fascinated.

Americans have either taken for granted, or maybe completely forgotten, the importance of conveying this message to our lover: "You are the center of the world to me." It's not that people from one country have a monopoly on how to convey that message, or that one way is better than another. Rather, it's that most countries aside from our own still convey the message.

What can we learn from other cultures? Are there romantic secrets the rest of the world knows that we don't? Is it possible to spice up our own special relationship by understanding the rituals of others?

This chapter was fun to research, and I hope will give you a few surprising ideas—ways to add a bit of international spice and spontaneity to your romantic lives. As we've just learned from our forays into the Hollywood of films, romance is fun—it's fantasy. There are infinite ways to express the love you feel for your romantic partner, and you can imaginatively cross the seas to find and effect some of the most interesting ones.

But we'll learn more than unfamiliar traditions. In nearly every culture but our own, people take time to practice the art of love. Sometimes it's unstructured time, like the long, late afternoons lovers spend with one another in Spain and Italy; sometimes it's highly structured time, like the intricately ordered tea ceremony shared by a Japanese husband and wife. But the messages lovers in many other cultures proclaim to one another are similar, and very often dissimilar to the message American lovers give to one another: the message in other cultures is "You are everything to me."

Something else is generally shared by cultures alien to our own, although it may be expressed in very different ways: romance in a wide variety of countries means restraint—and sometimes a step-by-step approach which would make the average, goal-oriented American impatient. I should quickly add that it's not my purpose to tear all of our own cultural practices down—we did give the world Marilyn Monroe, the bikini, and the Beach Boys, after all. But the prolonged romantic excitement which is prevalent elsewhere in the world is something Americans should take note of—and put to very pleasurable use.

There's another general difference between the American romantic approach and those of many other cultures, which may, at first, be a little harder to swallow. Male and female roles elsewhere in the world are often much more sharply delineated than they have become in this country. While that may raise our political hackles, it can add a high degree of erotic excitement: when a man and woman feel they have something very specific and very different to give one another, they truly fit as two halves of a whole. A woman desires what only a man can give her; a man desires a woman for the same reason. Not just in the obvious physical sense, but in an emotional sense as well. Romeo and Juliet were typically "Italian" in this way: it was for Romeo to woo Juliet, to climb the trellis to meet her. It would be unthinkable—certainly not Italian—for them to reverse roles. But as I have pointed out before, I'm calling for a romantic division of sex roles, not a political one. And we can take some very interesting international cues about how to make our romantic roles as exciting as possible.

Let's start with stereotypes. Is there such a thing, for example, as a Latin lover? There's certainly a cultural pressure for Spanish men, to draw from one Latin country, to play that role, says Dr. Michael Murphy, assistant professor of anthropology at the University of Alabama, in a recent article on international romance in *Self* magazine. "When a foreign woman comes to Spain," says Dr. Murphy, "she'll be besieged with compliments and sexual suggestions from Spanish men." Romantic and sexual ardor is bred into the very fabric of the Spanish male mind—an indication of machismo, the all-important virility aspired to by the typical Spanish man. This male braggadocio may not seem terribly appealing to the average American—but is it effective? Do women respond?

"I hate to admit it, and I usually don't," said Martha, a pretty Oklahoman who spent her junior year in college abroad in Madrid, "but I loved the attention! Not all the time—it gets wearing to get propositioned every time you walk out the door, but it certainly made me feel like an attractive woman. I was flattered more often than not." What about getting into a lasting relationship with a typical Spanish male? "Oh, that's not what they want. Especially not with an American woman—'American' means 'available' to Spanish men. But when I returned to the States, I have to say I missed that feeling of being special." Had she ever tried to recapture that feeling of being "special" in the eyes of a Spanish admirer—could she think of a way to arouse a similar ardor in an American man?

"It's funny," Martha said. "Now that I know that

kind of wooing is possible—that it goes on every day in Spain—I have looked for it in American men. It's not easy to find. But once—" Martha paused as she conjured up what was obviously a wonderful memory, "I did meet a 'Latin' man—not Spanish, but Portuguese-American." He invited her over to his apartment and had obviously carefully prepared for her arrival. Fado—haunting Portuguese music—played on the stereo, Portuguese wine was on the table; the room was lit by red candles. "My breath was taken away! It was like the best—the most romantic part—of my Spanish fantasies had come to life. Maybe it was the fact that he was half-American which made me feel safer than I did in Spain, that somehow tempered him in my eyes. But when, much later in the evening, after a beautiful dinner and laughing and talking, he kissed me—that's when I knew I wasn't with an American. The one thing a 'Latin' man knows how to do is touch a woman. It was incredible."

Whatever makes the touch of a Spanish, Italian, or French lover different from an American, it's more than technique. It comes from a whole way of viewing a man and a woman—touching is an extended moment, something to be cherished. Not only cherished, but built up to.

Even in the northern European countries—Scandinavia, Holland, and Germany—which in many ways seem as abrupt, industrial, and "American" as our own, there's a clear sense of restraint in the course of romance. Partially it's a lingering sense of Victorianism which psychologically regulates northern European behavior, but there's a real sense of politeness—of ritualized behavior—which dictates romance between men and women in this part of the world. We may not want to emulate this formality too closely, but we can learn from it.

"There's not the pressure to 'perform,'" said one Dutch correspondent, "that you have in America. In Holland, sex is not as immediate as it is in this country. We are not puritanical about sex, we simply see it as a very special activity. Jumping into bed immediately would not be pleasurable to men and women in Holland."

Taking time to know your romantic partner before having sex is the one universal I've found in the romantic practices of most European and Oriental cultures. Even in Sweden, regarded as a sexually "free" country, sexual freedom doesn't translate into promiscuity or unthinking sex. Dr. Deryck Calderwood, director of the Human Sexuality Program at New York University (cited in the *Self* article), calls Sweden a country "which enjoys one of the freest and most harmonious sexual attitudes of the civilized world"; in Sweden "sexuality is an inextricable part of daily life." There is, Dr. Calderwood says, "a more wholesome, matter-of-fact attitude toward the body and toward nudity. . . . As a result, sex there isn't fraught with negatives, or singled out as a problematic part of life—it's just one of the many aspects of being human."

The acceptance of sexuality in Sweden doesn't lead to disrespect of the human body or to wild orgies in the streets. But, healthy as the Swedish approach is, is it "romantic"?

"Perhaps not in the conventional sense of moonlight and champagne," said Katherine, an American woman married to Lars, a Swede, "but I can't think of a more romantic life than Lars and I had when we lived in Stockholm. We thought nothing of taking saunas in the nude with our friends, or swimming nude at pools. Children, men, and women—everyone was used to the sight of nudity. What this exposure did for Lars and me was wonderful. In a sense our passion for each other never ceased. It was gently there all day long. It was as if the whole atmosphere was softly erotic. And when we finally did make love, it came as the most natural and beautiful part of our day. To me, that's the essence of romance—that naturalness, that ease."

A gentler and more protracted approach to love also allows time for sensuality. Perhaps no culture enjoys the pleasures of the senses more than the French—at least, no culture has as refined an enjoyment of smell, touch, and taste. "Scent is all-important to me," said Marie-Celeste, a Parisian-born artist who spends time equally in New York and France. "To me the more natural, the better. The subtle scent of a man I love in my arms, the scent I know he loves from me. Only the barest touch of perfume is needed to bring this out. Sometimes no perfume at all." Marie-Celeste met me on one of her trips to New York; she was with her lover, Philippe, a Frenchman. It was obvious they were in love. Philippe's eyes all but made love to her every time she spoke. "Michel," she explained to her lover, "is writing a book on romance." Philippe looked at me astonished: "What could an American possibly know about romance?" I was too amused to take offense—plus here I had two live Parisians ready to tell me everything! "I have one word of advice," Philippe said. "No after-shave lotion! *C'est une abomination.*" Marie-Celeste laughed and nuzzled her lover's neck.

The average American's distaste for natural body odor is something Marie-Celeste and Philippe found very silly. They knew, as all the French seem to, how erotic a freshly washed—but unperfumed—human scent can be.

Food is also an occasion for romance in France—as it is, to the same degree, in Italy. The cuisines of both countries, in fact, say much about their romantic approaches. "It is not surprising," Marie-Celeste informed me, "that Americans eat so much fast food. It is the way most of them make love." The subtleties of classic French cuisine—the gentle mingling of flavors and carefully selected ingredients are, to Marie-Celeste, a precise reflection of the way Parisians, especially, feel about love. It is no wonder France is the country whose name is given to a very special kiss.

The simplicity of much of Italian cooking—the bright colors and the flavors of its fresh ingredients—perhaps makes an even bolder statement about the culture it nourishes. The concept of serenading a lover is largely an Italian one—bold, beseeching, passionate song: so it is with food. I find an Italian meal one of the most romantic occasions I can imagine. The cuisine, like the culture, embraces you boldly, memorably. In fact, some of the most romantic writing I've read comes from Italian cookbooks! Here, for example, is Marcella Hazan, making an analogy between cooking and music (she could as easily be talking about romance):

> Music and cooking are so much alike. There are people who, simply by working hard at it, become technically quite accomplished at either art. But it isn't until one connects technique to feeling, turning it into the outward thrust of that feeling, that one becomes a musician, or a cook.

Or a lover.

I dwell on the romantic message food can convey because it's one of the easiest ways to create a romantic event. The sharing of a simple, sensual meal makes a perfect expression of romance—and prelude to love. Plan a French or Italian evening with your lover—make it simple and as "authentic" as you can. How will you know if you've created an authentically French or Italian meal and evening? If it feels like making love, you'll have succeeded.

No one I've spoken with is more aware of the romantic quality that is created by a wonderful meal than Antonio, who works for an import company. Antonio was born and raised in Italy and now lives in New York City. Yet, his extended visits to Japan for business have given him a deep appreciation of the Oriental respect for ritual. His view of both Japanese and American culture is all the more interesting since he was raised in the atmosphere that is probably the most opposite, at least on the surface, to the Oriental one.

"The more technologically oriented and industrially proficient a country," he told me, "the greater that culture's need to get back in touch with people, and most certainly a lover. The Japanese, for example, probably the most technologically oriented nation today, separate their workday from their home life. I lived with a 'high-tech' Japanese businessman and his family during my last stay in Kyoto. After work, Norio would sit with his wife and quietly become involved with origami, the art of paper folding. It seemed as though this time together allowed each to adjust to one another after a typically frantic business day apart."

The degree of ritual involved in origami, in kirigami (paper cutting), in the Japanese tea ceremeony, in bonsai (the ceremony of cultivating miniature trees), or in ikebana (the ceremony of flower arrangement), to name a few, is daunting even to modern Japanese. The beauty of these rituals is breath-taking. As with the rituals of any other country, I'm not suggesting re-creating them to the letter. But I am suggesting that we look at the culture's motivation for, and mode of, performing them for deeper clues. Respect and love are deeply bound in Japanese relationships, a coalescence which may warrant emulating.

Nowhere is the sense of romance and restraint more exquisite and more profoundly pleasurable than with the rituals learned and practiced by the geisha.

For centuries, the geisha represented the art of love-making at its highest and most refined. Geishas existed solely to provide pleasure to their patrons—and the arts of giving these pleasures took years to learn. It was not just a mastery of physical love-making which was the geisha's goal—although that art was important—but of music and conversation. The geisha appealed to all a patron's sensibilities—physical, mental, even spiritual. The geisha's legacy is felt in Japanese marriages even today: the willowy (and always kimono-clad) courtesans represented on ancient Japanese woodblock prints present a standard of female beauty which Japanese women continue to seek to emulate. It was, and is, considered unsexy for a woman to appear nude. The mystery provided by the soft drapery of a kimono is far more erotic to the Japanese than an unclothed body possibly could be. Harmony with nature is perhaps the strongest philosophical tenet of the Japanese; accordingly, the geisha—and modern Japanese women who are influenced by the ideal of the geisha—make a kind of total love to a man, soothing mind and spirit as well as body and thus tantalizing and satisfying in a thousand different ways.

Another Japanese ritual, the tea ceremony, is perhaps the most vivid example of the shared responsibilities of a Japanese couple. It is also an event of surpassing beauty.

Few descriptions of this ceremony do the kind of justice to it which James Clavell provided in *Shogun*. Here, Clavell describes the tea ceremony which the character of Buntaro performs for his wife, Mariko:

> In the peace and quiet of the little house, Buntaro fastidiously opened the small earthenware tea caddy of the T'ang dynasty and, with equal care, took up the bamboo spoon, beginning the final part of the ceremony. Deftly he spooned up exactly the right amount of green powder and put it into the handleless porcelain cup. An ancient cast-iron kettle was singing over the charcoal. . .

Buntaro prepared the tea meticulously and bowed to his wife, who knelt before him, and he offered her the cup.

> She bowed and took it with equal refinement, admiring the green liquid, and sipped three times, rested, then sipped again, finishing it. . . .She begged him to taste the cha himself, as was expected of her. He sipped. . . .

The ceremony continued with equal symmetry. Finally:

With great care, ritually he washed and dried the cup, using the peerless cotton cloth, and laid both in their places. He bowed to her and she to him. The cha-no-yu was finished. . . . "You were truly a master tonight, Buntaro-san. You gave me so much happiness. . . . Everything was perfect for me, the garden and how you used artistry to overcome the flaws with light and shadow. . . . Everything perfect, even the character you'd written on the towel, ai—affection. For me tonight, affection was the perfect word."

This description captures for me the essence of what Japanese men and women traditionally have sought to provide each other: a display of affection and respect, exacting in its detail, which represents to an almost final degree the principles we've been exploring throughout this book.

After doing research for this chapter and speaking to many people from different countries, I now understand a type of romantic harmony or balance of which before I had only the vaguest sense. It is important for each of us to take the initiative in telling and showing our lover that we care; sometimes, though, holding back not only makes for a change of pace but actually may be the best way to show your affection. I now understand, for instance, why most of us are so turned off by the person who declares his or her love very early in a relationship. I'm not saying that love at first sight does not exist. But often, hearing those important three words, "I love you," too soon makes most of us justifiably suspicious: How often does he—or she—say this and to how many people?

Romance is a ritual that expresses affection. Everything from lusty Italian food to the languor of a French boudoir to the intricacies of the tea ceremony described above can give any two lovers innumerable clues.

To the question first asked in this chapter—"Are they doing anything we aren't?"—I hope we can eventually answer, "Not anymore." I'm not saying you've got to go out and learn a new language or how to prepare Japanese tea or Italian pasta; I am suggesting that we learn to express our romantic feelings with the same care, attention to detail, and *joie de vivre* as our neighbors to the north, east, south, and west of us.

13

Now That We're "One," Why Are We So Bored?

HERE'S THE CLINCHER. You're now a couple. You eat, talk, sleep, kiss, and spend time with one another as imaginatively as you can. You bring home roses on a rainy Monday after work; you surprise your lover with a kiss on the neck in an elevator when nobody is looking; you leave lovely romantic notes in unexpected places— on the bathroom mirror, under the pillow; you've spent hours looking into each other's eyes by candlelight.

Months of this have passed. And one day you wake up and feel you've run dry. Slowly little things begin to bother you way out of proportion to their significance. She still leaves the cap off the toothpaste. He's still piling up his dirty socks on the bedroom floor. The story you found so funny the first time your lover told it gets told once too often at yet another party: you feel you'll scream if you hear it again. You don't want to give up. You may try to recapture the fun you once had—you may feel there's got to be some novelty that hasn't occurred to either of you—something to bring the excitement, the zip, the interest back to your lives. But nothing occurs to you.

Months of being with the person you love most, and you're bored.

We've explored any number of ways to spice up our romantic lives, and if there's an underlying theme it's that by paying attention, by making your time together special, by being as sensitive as you can be to the feelings and desires of your lover, you're doing more than developing new and unusual "techniques": you're developing a romantic "attitude." A concert pianist or champion tennis player doesn't practice hours a day only to drum in technique: their practice pays off in subtler ways. Immersing yourself in music or sport or another person means developing a sixth sense: it becomes natural for you to come up with your own innovations; it's natural to think and respond even when you're not conscious of doing so. A pianist may come up with his own, surprising interpretation of a piece; a tennis pro may come up with a combination of moves nobody's ever tried before. And a lover used to being romantic will find the same ease in sparking and resparking love—he or she has developed an attitude which tells how.

Technique may be able to save a moment, but attitude can save a whole relationship.

It's essential to point this out here. Because as much as I advocate imagination, play, surprising tricks and techniques which can get you to experience new romantic delights, you can't rely on these techniques alone to keep your love alive. A woman correspondent's tale of exhaustion made this point especially clear.

Alice went on one of those "cruises to nowhere"

which have recently become so popular. A luxurious ocean liner departed from the New York harbor, traveled enough miles away from shore so that the casinos on board could be operated legally, and sailed down to some point they were told was off Cape Hatteras before returning. "We might have traveled in a wide circle off New Jersey as far as I knew," wrote Alice. "No land was ever visible, and it truly felt we were going nowhere." Alice eventually found herself going nowhere in another sense. "This was, as you'd expect, a singles trip, and you've never seen so many activities crammed into a weekend of sailing—about six meals a day, movies at all hours, shuffleboard, skeet shooting, co-ed dancercize classes, cocktail and masquerade parties—you name it." At the first "get acquainted" party Alice soon got acquainted with a handsome man named Rick. Rick was a dynamo. "As many scheduled activities as there were on board," Alice said, "they weren't enough for Rick. I had fun—it was incredible to feel his energy, and not a moment wasn't filled with something fun and exciting. Rick didn't stop with the scheduled events—he gave parties in his cabin, sometimes just for the two of us, sometimes inviting other people he'd met. Talk about a whirlwind romance—I'm still dizzy from it."

Alice had a "terrific" time, she said, and she was genuinely fond of Rick—everything he did was calculated to please her. She didn't expect to see him after the cruise, however—Rick was the kind of guy, she thought, who let loose for a weekend and then receded from whomever he'd decided to let loose with afterwards. But Alice was wrong.

"After we docked back in New York, he was insistent about seeing me again," she said. "And he did. Boy, did he see me!" Alice's new beau called her in the mornings before she went to work, several times a day at the office, after she returned home, and late at night. "I didn't have time to think," she said. "I found myself going out with him as many nights as we could manage—during the week and on weekends—and after a month or so he said it was silly to live apart, we were obviously in love, so why didn't we move in together?" Alice was still being swept off her feet. "I've never been wooed with such vengeance."

She thought that surely once they'd moved in with one another their lives would calm down a bit. But they didn't. "Rick was romantically hyperactive. He'd meet me wearing a funny mask when I least expected it, or cook an elaborate Chinese meal in the middle of the night; once he even dressed up in a gorilla suit and pretended I was Fay Wray in *King Kong*. He never let up. After two months of this I felt I was living with some wildly wound-up Martian. Mork had nothing on Rick."

Rick's attentions were genuine enough. He really seemed crazy about Alice in his hyperactive way. And the romantic techniques we've been exploring in this book—everything from Hollywood to Tokyo—don't begin to suggest what Rick was able to devise with his effusive imagination.

"But finally," Alice said, "I'd had enough. It wasn't only that I was exhausted from his attentions. It's that I never had the chance—the time—to figure out what I really felt about Rick. Then it dawned on me that that's exactly what Rick didn't want me to have—time to think, and maybe doubt. I began to really resent this."

On one Saturday morning, with Rick pulling at her to go to Coney Island and ride on the roller coaster, Alice finally said no. She said no to more than Coney Island— she said she had to get away for the weekend alone. Rick looked at her blankly. He simply couldn't comprehend what Alice was doing.

Alice found herself in a terribly awkward position; she had no desire to hurt Rick, but she felt strangled by his attentions—and, ironically, bored with their too many activities. "I tried to tell him that I wasn't sure if we had a relationship beneath all our 'fun.' He recoiled like a hurt animal. 'But we spend all our time together!' he said. 'Doesn't that show we have a relationship?' I soon saw he was frightened—deathly frightened—of silence, of peace. But I couldn't get him to admit it."

Rick was on a crazy treadmill—full of ideas and energy and fear, and going nowhere. There wasn't anything substantial in his relationships because he felt so insubstantial himself. "I wish I could say I was able to reach him, get him to quiet down and trust himself, trust me, but I couldn't," Alice wrote. She finally did leave Rick— for good. "As far as I know, he's swept some other woman off her feet and is at it again. But you can't live like that. You can't help falling back to earth. If only Rick would let himself do that."

In his own way, Rick was a master of romantic technique. But he left out the essence of romance, without which all the technique in the world becomes nothing but empty gesture: he never truly gave himself to the relationship.

I dwell on this unusual example of romantic boredom because it is unusual. Boredom in relationships doesn't often come from the excess of one partner's attentions. But Rick's and Alice's example is a useful introduction to the problem of boredom because it points out that an excess of romantic gesture is as potentially damaging as a lack of it. Attention has to be meaningful to be effective. All the flowers, wine, and candlelight in the world can't disguise a lover who isn't truly giving himself. For a while, romantic "noise" may block awareness that there's no deep feeling behind it. But if your gestures are hollow, fearful, and a cover-up, your partner will eventually see and feel it. Boredom won't be the only problem that emerges in that lover's response—pain and a sense of betrayal come right alongside. The key? Allow the course of your love to make you more vulnerable, not less. Trust that you don't have to fill up your time busily, meaninglessly. A relationship can't last without that mutual trust—that it's okay to be who you are quietly, at your most naked. Alice longed for a real touch, a quiet gesture, that she hoped Rick would be capable of giving. But reaching out that way takes courage, the courage to be silent—a courage Rick sadly lacked.

When we investigated the art of dating before, we saw how important it is to give. Here again, giving is the key to overcoming boredom in a longer-term relationship. Sometimes this means giving in a literal sense—special things you make or buy and surprise a lover with. You're in a special position with someone you've lived with for a long time: you know better than anyone else what will please, what's needed.

One example, out of many, of this "intimate" giving comes to mind: Derek is a friend of mine whose father died unexpectedly several years ago. One day Derek accidentally dropped and shattered a porcelain shaving mug he'd inherited from his father. That mug meant a lot to Derek, and he keenly felt a symbolic loss. About a year later, Elaine, his wife, happened to pass an antique store and saw the mug's duplicate in the window. She was thrilled—she knew how much it would mean to Derek to have his father's mug replaced. She rushed into the store to buy it: it turned out to be very expensive—it cost more money than she had with her, and more than she felt her budget would allow. But she swallowed hard and decided a week or two of noodle casseroles and hot dogs wouldn't kill anybody. Elaine put down a deposit on the mug, went to the bank for more money, and returned to purchase it. She then left the mug in the bathroom—in the same place the original had been. The next morning her husband saw the mug; he walked quietly from the bathroom into the bedroom and lay down beside his wife. "You're incredible," Derek said to her. There were tears in his eyes.

Again, you're in a special position to please someone you've known for years. Realize that you know things about your lover that nobody else possibly could. Learning to use that intimate knowledge can't help but deepen a relationship. Boredom is out of the question when you act and give sensitively.

This doesn't mean that you have to limit yourself to gestures or gifts you know will please your lover; without excesses like Rick's, there's nothing like a well-timed surprise to jostle you out of a rut. One woman I met on an airplane (I was in the middle of a lecture tour), when she found out I was writing this book, couldn't wait to tell me what her husband had recently done for her. Her name was Julie, and she described what happened at the end of a week during which she admitted she'd been "hell" to live with. It was one of those classic weeks when everything that could go wrong did: her car broke down, she had dozens of difficult clients at her personnel management job, and it rained every day. She was depressed and snappy with her husband, Craig, who at least had the good sense to stay out of her way during most of her rampages. Friday came along, and she got home from work at six o'clock, as usual. But she dreaded the thought of having to make dinner, having to do anything! Julie started to feel as if her life was one long series of unpleasant ruts.

Then she heard Craig call, "Honey?" from the bedroom.

"Waddya want?" was her testy reply.

"Would you come in here a minute, please?" he called back.

She marched into the bedroom and gasped. The room was completely filled with balloons! Floor to ceiling, in, around, and under the bed. She could barely spot Craig in the center of them all.

"I don't know how these things got in here," he said, "but could you help me get rid of at least the ones under the covers?" She waded through the mass of fat, colored balloons to the bed, and saw Craig grinning goofily, one hand on the neck of a champagne bottle. And she helped him get rid of the balloons under the covers, laughing and relieved that, of all the men in the world she might have married, she'd picked Craig.

Craig's surprise "gift" was an impressive feat of romantic engineering—it took all day to blow up those balloons!—but it was also wonderful because it was a risk. Julie might have walked in and yelled about the mess, in the mood she'd been in! Sometimes taking a gamble, acting on an educated guess, can get a relationship on a new track. It's important to be vulnerable, not just in the sense of confessing your heart but in acting in ways you hope will show your lover you care. That's the difference between Craig and Rick: Rick went on automatic pilot. But Craig's whole purpose in his crazy balloon idea was to make his wife happy, to cheer her up.

Moral? Take the risk of making your lover laugh when you know he or she needs it most.

Boredom is as insidious as it's occasionally unavoidable. The main trouble about being in a rut isn't only the rut itself: it's that when you feel you can predict everything about a person or a relationship, you can't conceive of a way out. The symptoms of boredom are many: you may pay less attention to your home, to your meals together, or you may even let your body go to seed. Boredom, like depression, often deepens if you cannot imagine ever escaping the rut.

Sometimes stopping that pattern means giving to yourself. I'm one of those people who believe that clothes do come close to making the man—and woman. Not only clothes, but exercise, physical activity. It's not within the scope of this book to outline a regimen of physical exercise, and it may seem a somewhat odd topic to drag into our discussion of romance. But since romantic boredom so often leads to not taking care of yourself (not to mention your lover), taking measure of your appearance more than warrants a mention here. The first thing to remember is that you can often stem the tide of boredom in a relationship by eliminating the boredom you feel toward yourself.

I once knew a very bright and articulate couple who'd been married for about twelve years, had two small kids, and lived in a large apartment in Philadelphia. When they'd first moved in, the apartment was absolutely beautiful—the care that went into it reflected the care they lavished on each other. Italian antiques Anthony had inherited were polished to an intense glow by Marian, his wife. They both looked physically wonderful, too. They were terribly in love, and they kept themselves attractive not only out of a desire to please each other, but because they felt so good about themselves. But as the years went by, their home and their lives and finally even the way they looked grew shabby. Anthony went through a series of advertising jobs in a very weak market—money was scarce and taking care of their two kids drained Marian to the core. They found themselves on a downward spiral of boredom and depression which manifested itself in a thousand different ways: not least in how they looked.

Finally one of Marian's closest friends commented on the fact that she didn't look healthy, and that it wouldn't be a bad idea to take off a little weight. Marian was shocked—and then realized that her friend was right. She'd avoided looking at herself too closely in the mirror; there didn't seem to be any reason to. Anthony's lovemaking had long ago become perfunctory; she supposed she looked "all right" and was prepared to accept that. But her friend got her to think, and she finally came to the decision to pay a little attention to herself. She joined an inexpensive exercise program in a nearby YWCA which didn't demand too much of her time, and slowly the activity began to have an effect, not only carving off a few pounds but getting Marian to think of herself as an attractive woman. She began paying more attention to her hair and her clothes as well as to her body. She even began cleaning the house with more care.

It wasn't long before Anthony noticed, although at first he couldn't quite put his finger on the difference. It was as if Marian had become more animated, more alive. And, in an initially subtle and then a literally measurable way (she lost ten unwanted pounds in several weeks), she was turning into a very beautiful woman again. The inevitable happened: Anthony took a hard look at his flabby waistline and decided to make some changes in his own life. Marian was delighted when he announced, one day after work, that he'd joined the gym.

"What's happening to us?" Marian asked. "We're not bored anymore!"

The point isn't only that gritting your teeth and deciding to discipline yourself physically a little will make you more attractive to your lover and to yourself, but that sometimes the efforts of one partner to improve his or her own life can carry over to the other. Hitting the rock bottom of boredom can breed this turnaround—something's got to change, you feel, and if you're lucky you realize you can start to change things—immediately.

Some amount of boredom may be inevitable in a relationship which lasts long enough to feel "comfortable," but there's never a time you can't take up the reins again and "travel" to a more interesting, more productive, and more romantic place. This may mean slowing down from an excess of activity to find the meaning of who you are and who your lover is; it may mean shaking up a routine you suddenly realize has engulfed you and your lover; it may mean allowing yourself to hear a silent cry of need from your lover or yourself, and then having the courage to do something about it.

You may, in fact, have to accept aspects of yourself and your lover that you realize won't—or can't—change. A recent study, conducted by the University of Toronto, of 129 couples married longer than twenty-five years attempted to discover the secret of relationship longevity. Most of what they found was to be expected: these couples believed in commitment, kindness, good manners— all the values they grew up with. But one finding deserves our special attention: don't expect perfection from your partner.

Your lover may have what seems to be a congenital inability to put the cap back on the toothpaste tube. But look a little wider and a little deeper. There's a lot you haven't had the pleasure of discovering yet—a lifetime of surprises.

In the next chapter we'll meet two lovely people who have made that mutual discovery—and continue to make it every moment of their lives.

14

True Partnership: The Final Frontier

ACCORDING TO a recent survey, more people are getting married today than in many years. There's a reason for the swing back to marriage: more people hope for a kind of satisfaction they've not been able to find in any other union. I'm not saying this means the divorce rate is going to magically plummet: the hope for satisfaction in a lifelong relationship often remains exactly that—a hope. Marriage, as you've heard any number of experts tell you, is hard work. But the rewards can be fantastic—feelings more deeply satisfying than those any other association can bring.

Or so say many of the married couples with whom I've spoken.

The University of Toronto study of 129 married couples I cited in the last chapter may seem a little bland in its findings. The main message seems to be that people get and stay married because they want to, and because they subscribe to what we may think of as old-fashioned values: they believe in commitment, respect, kindness and love. What those general words don't convey is the *passion* of commitment felt by couples who stay together for twenty-five years or more. This is a kind of passion that just can't exist in fledgling relationships.

Perhaps this is the biggest surprise about marriage. Isn't the first flush of desire, the head-over-heels feeling we've talked about as quintessentially romantic—isn't this the strongest romantic emotion a person could possibly feel? Doesn't everything subsequent pale by comparison?

Meet one couple who thinks not. Al and Frances are, respectively, sixty-four and sixty years old. They've been married for thirty-four years and live in a small town in Connecticut—rural but close enough to New York City that they can get in to see a Broadway show, attend a concert or go to an art gallery when they feel the occasional urban lure. Al is an attorney; Frances a commercial artist who's finally found the time to turn to her real interest—watercolors. In the past several years she's become impressively successful with her painting. She sells continually at local art shows, a nice addition to their income and a source of unending pride to Al.

"Look how good she's getting!" Al said to me one evening when they invited me over for dinner. He was pointing to a broad seascape, a stormy mixture of grays and blues, sky and water battling for attention. "You can almost feel the spray, can't you?" Al was beaming. Frances poked her head into the living room. She's a beautiful woman, silver haired and with a strong classical face—a serene face. "Stop talking about how good I'm getting and come to dinner," she informed her husband with mock impatience. "Always telling me what to do," Al grumbled.

We walked into the dining room, the table softly lit with candles, a steaming casserole in the center. There was a wonderful light in Al's eyes—a mirthful light—as if he were sharing something secret and funny with Frances while talking to me. They had both dressed for dinner, although it was a Monday night and no special occasion—I'm an old friend of the family, so they certainly weren't trying to impress me. Al wore an ascot ("I keep telling him they went out of style about forty years ago," Frances said) and jacket; Frances an elegant black dress. Al carefully held his wife's chair as she seated herself, and gently helped her closer to the table. "I don't know how you do it," he said. "Getting all this stuff hot and on the table at the same time." "If you'd gotten here on time, it would have been hotter!" Frances informed him. "Isn't she terrible?" Al said to me, his eyes glowing with that same extraordinary light.

Al poured us all a glass of white wine—an Italian Soave he said they'd just picked up on sale, but it glittered as brightly as any more expensive vintage in the candlelight and warmth of these two long-time lovers.

What's most extraordinary to me about Al and Frances isn't just the romantic detail they give to every moment they share, but the feeling I had sitting with them: the bond of their love was almost visible. Sitting across from one another at the table, they were connected in some magical, unfaltering way I've rarely felt between two people. How did they achieve this? They knew about this book, and they undoubtedly expected the question from me.

"About fifteen years of throwing lamps at each other," was Al's first quip.

"He can't put that in his book!" Frances chided him.

"Come on—tell me." If there is a secret to "relationship longevity," Al and Frances knew it, and I was bent on finding it out.

Frances ran her finger around the base of her wineglass.

"I think," she began, "it's because we've learned to make every moment count. Believe me, that wasn't easy." Frances raised her eyebrows and aimed an ironic smile at Al. "We've been through so much together," she continued, "as much pain as joy—and for so many years. I can't imagine knowing anyone better than I know Al—I can't imagine depending on anyone more."

"I'll tell you our secret," Al chimed in. "We never look back."

"Of course we look back!" Frances disagreed. "There's so much to remember!"

"You've always had a better memory than I," her husband replied.

Frances' first comment gives a new meaning to the word "relationship," a word with which I've never been comfortable: it seems to describe something singular and static. It doesn't imply the reality of what two people are to one another—two individuals who continually change. When Frances said that she and Al had learned to "make every moment count," she was revealing a great deal. Frances knows that life—and her marriage—only exists as a series of moments, and that what happens in a moment influences moments to come. I said before that marriage took work and it does, but it's a lot more subtle than digging ditches.

Al gives a clue to what this "work" entails: "we never look back." Both Al and Frances give each moment of their married lives direction, not only directing their energies toward each other, but directing their whole marriage forward. Much is implied by "not looking back": the ability to forgive, the ability to take joy in the present, the ability to envision a satisfying and workable future.

And yet this looking forward is tempered by Frances' assertion: "there's so much to remember!" We are the product of who we've been. Although Al made light of his ability to remember, I know from so many stories he's shared with me about his years with Frances that his memory is not only very sharp, but provides a real function in his life with Frances today. Sharing your past— remembering it—brings you to an intimate and nurturing union. You're in a special situation with someone with whom you've lived for a long time: that person not only knows who you are now, but knows to a large degree what experiences have formed you.

Finally, what Al and Frances revealed to me—not only by their words, but by their lives—is that they've made a real commitment to staying together, a commitment that is strengthened every moment of their lives. Much of what people say they fear about sexual and emotional monogamy is that it's "restrictive." But it's within the bounds of these "restrictions" that you may find your greatest freedom.

Dr. Ralph I. Hyatt in his book *Before You Love Again* is

clear about the importance of commitment in any long-term union: "To commit is to give yourself to marriage without reservations. You can't say, 'Well, if this doesn't work, I can get out,' and expect a marriage to work. You can't say, 'Well, I'll keep that marriage vow, but not the other.'"

Dr. Hyatt also illuminates what often happens when you decide to renege on one or another marriage vow in the interest of more "freedom": "There is no way to successfully fake this commitment. You can't say one thing and do another without paying a price. That people do so does not really mean they get by with it. They pay a psychic price (psychologists call it *cognitive dissonance*) if nothing else, or they reap a divorce."

The "psychic price" we pay when we knowingly betray a lover—or a spouse—is enormous. While we may be chafing at one particular bit or another, sneaking away and being dishonestly "free," all too often this leads to the opposite feeling: being trapped by our own deceptiveness. There is nothing more boring or more damaging than a lie, especially one you've allowed to creep into a relationship with someone you love. That's another lesson Al and Frances have taught me: that commitment truly felt and nurtured allows you, in fact encourages you, to be truthful. There is nothing I can imagine Al and Frances not sharing with one another, because they've seen to it there's nothing they'd ever do to betray or hurt each c her.

In a sense, marriage is the ultimate outcome of romance. The caring, sensitivity, imagination, and trust which romance inevitably includes are exactly the traits which make a marriage successful. As we've seen in any number of stories throughout this book, you'll have times with your lover when you feel like exploding in anger, when you're bored out of your skull, when you feel deeply misunderstood. Al and Frances would be the first to admit they were no strangers to those feelings.

But the fragile plant they've planted and nurtured and coaxed from seedling to tree—their marriage—has finally become stronger than any of the storms it inevitably had to weather.

Each of us is capable of planting—and raising—that same tree. Marriage, like the romance that nurtures it, offers a promise and a fulfillment open to all of us.

Epilogue

WHEN WE LOOK back on the 1980s from the perspective of ten or twenty years, what label will we have given the decade? We've divided the rest of the twentieth century into neat little ten-year segments—an artificial division, perhaps, but not entirely unhelpful. The fifties did, for example, mark a period of sexual and emotional repression; the sixties had an undeniable "revolutionary" effect. And, in attempting to lick at our wounds in the seventies, we did arguably create a "me" decade.

It seems to me that there are two contradictory trends today which are already defining our experience of the eighties. In fact, two major magazines recently ran cover stories which point out this dichotomy: *Time* magazine's "Is the Sexual Revolution Over?" and *Esquire's* "Men and Their Money: The Passion of the Eighties." As I've said before, the more sophisticated our technology, the more abstract and formidable our computer-dominated world, the greater our need for human intimacy becomes. *Time* says we're turning to each other romantically in ways we haven't expressed in twenty years—monogamy and marriage are no longer the dirty words they once were. Part of this trend is perhaps the inevitable pendulum effect: we're starving for the kind of affection and closeness the sexual revolution couldn't deliver. But part of our need for romance is in response to the technological, profit-oriented world the *Esquire* article describes. As we saw in the "Love and Money" chapter, you can't love a job (or a computer) in the way you can love another human being. Our need for each other has never been more deeply felt.

If the 1980s becomes a decade of "New Romanticism," it's a label I wouldn't mind. So many people feel such pain, such longing to discover how to love one another again. It is my conviction that romance provides the guidelines for teaching us how to find love and keep love alive.

Romance is a broad attitude with any number of variations—it is an attitude which can help us ease our way back into each other's arms and lives. I promised you a varied journey in this book, but if you walk away with one piece of advice from *A Return to Romance*, I hope it will be this: find yourself in the heart of another human being and learn the strength of human beings' single most powerful trait—the ability to love.

Romance is the most effective guide I know to reaching that destination; I can promise you it will take you on the most wonderful journey of your life.